The Journey Called YOU

A Roadmap

to Self-Discovery and Acceptance

Julie Fuimano, MBA, BSN, RN

Live your greatness!

Julie Fuimano

Nurturing Your Success Publications
MALVERN, PENNSYLVANIA

First printing 2005

ISBN 0-9765605-3-4   LCCN 2005923284

**ATTENTION CORPORATIONS, UNIVERSITIES, COLLEGES, AND
PROFESSIONAL ORGANIZATIONS:** Quantity discounts are available on
bulk purchases of this book for educational, gift purposes, or as premiums for
increasing magazine subscriptions or renewals. Special books or book excerpts
can also be created to fit specific needs. For information, please contact
Nurturing Your Success Publications, Chester County Commons, 4 Mystic Lane,
Malvern, PA 19355; (800) 977-6878; www.TheJourneyCalledYOU.com.

Dedication

In memory of
John Fuimano,
whose presence in my life
made a huge impact
in my personal evolution.

And to my son,
Joshua,
sheer joy, who adds richness
and depth to my life
beyond compare.

Table of Contents

Chapter One

Starting Your Journey 1

Understanding the journey of self-discovery and acceptance and how to read the book.

Chapter Two

Getting to the "Who" 9

In order to start the journey into who you are, you need to understand what is meant by "who."

    What

        A Walk Through the Clouds: Minimizing

    Why

        A Walk Through the Clouds: The Blame Game

        A Walk Through the Clouds: The "Why Me" Trap

    How

    Coaching Note: Understanding Commitment

    Who

    Coaching Note: Teaching Children to Make Good Choices

    Coaching Challenge

Foreword

by Lori M. Weiner

I remember it so clearly: It was four years ago. She called me after being laid off from her third job. "This doesn't feel right," she said. "I'm meant to be doing something more. What do you think I'm meant to be doing?"

Here's someone, with more initials after her last name than I have letters in my first name, asking me what I think her career path should be. The first words I spoke were "You are great at helping others."

It's a passion she has, a gift you might say. She likes to challenge people, have them think about reaching the next level of their life's journey. After all, the last several years she spent in human resources, talking with people about their careers. Now it was her turn to take her career to the next level.

My sister, Julie Fuimano, opened Nurturing Your Success in 2001. It was a perfect name for the business she wanted to develop. She was going to make this journey work. Through determination, life's experiences, and focus she was going to succeed.

This book has been in Julie's thoughts for quite some time. She wants you to challenge yourself, believe in yourself, and see all that you are and reach for what you are meant to be.

Take your time while reading this book. It is not a novel to race through. Spend time at the end of each chapter answering the questions. Remember this is the road of discovery to YOU. Some of the questions will be internally difficult to face. Face them head-on, with ambition and determination.

You are worth it!

Soaring

by Lori Weiner

It was a clear day
Showing off a very blue sky.
I could see for miles and
Could picture myself flying—soaring.
I did not know then where
This journey of flight would take me.
But I felt calmness.
And then it appeared.
It appeared so clearly,
The truth right in front of me.
This journey was me—
Me trusting me.

Preface

"You are so much more than you will ever know. Spend your life wondering over the most important asset in your life—*you*."

Throughout our teenage years, we begin our quest for finding our identity and getting to know ourselves: Who am I? Who am I going to be? What will I do with my life? How can I learn to be myself and to accept myself? And is that going to be good enough? Will I be able to live up to the expectations that others have of me?

That's when my journey began. When I entered my teen years, I started wondering what this thing called 'life' was all about. "Why are we here? What am I supposed to do? How does one do this *life* thing and how will I know if I'm doing it right?"

Because no one else was asking these questions publicly, I thought I was the only one who didn't know. I thought the mystery to life was this big secret and I was being kept out of the loop. I spent years doing things the wrong way, losing myself to drugs and living my life completely off course. I knew there was another path—a better path— for me to travel, but someone had forgotten to give me the roadmap or any clear instructions. I had absolutely no idea how to find this path and worse, I had no idea of the destination! Drugs were one way I could escape the confusion inside me, even though I knew this wasn't the life I wanted to live. After all, the only place drug use gets you is into an early grave. I just didn't know who I was or who I wanted to be. And I didn't really know how to be comfortable with myself.

The teenage years are a time for determining your identity, discovering who you are. It's no wonder that so many people fumble during these years. Many adults are still asking these very questions, so how can we expect our kids to learn if we're still struggling with our own identities? Peer pressure, parental pressure, academic performance as well as competition in sports and other clubs easily distract you from the inner work of discovering the kind of person you want to be. You're so busy "doing" and performing that learning how to "be" is just something that's not discussed. And even though you might have an idea of who you are, when you're that young, how do you learn to listen to your own heart when everyone is telling you what to do? Without a guide, mentor, role model, or coach, it's extremely difficult to come through the teenage years unscathed.

For me, the early twenties were bewildered years; I floated through my first college degree trying to find something that I liked. I chose a college that had some 30,000-plus students so it was easy for me to get lost in the crowd. I had no direction or clear identity; and I felt very alone. It took eight long years to finally complete my first bachelor's degree in business administration after changing majors at least four times. I thought that I had to know what I was going to do with the rest of my life in choosing my degree. I wish someone would have shared that this was just the grounding I would need to get started. The adult world was still so new and I didn't yet know how to navigate my way.

As a young adult, you experience a shift where you realize that you're an adult and everything that word signifies becomes true. It's at that moment when you discover you're just like everyone else. You're no longer a child—you've entered the next stage of life. You must accept responsibility for yourself, for your life, for your choices—for the direction your life takes. You are free to do whatever you want (or whatever you *think* you want) and to chart your own course. This is a profound moment for people and one that's often unacknowledged and not celebrated. What age you are when this occurs is not nearly as important as the moment in which you embrace who you're becoming in the continuum of life.

The other big shift that occurs during your young adult years is the shift from seeking the approval of others (usually parents or other authority figures) to approving of oneself. This shift is often delayed and many people find themselves still seeking outside approval for the choices they make well into their thirties, forties, even fifties. Clearly, the sooner you can make this shift, the sooner you start living your own life and take back your power to create the life you want, rather than what other people expect for you.

Years passed and I learned more about me. After all, you can only learn so much from watching others; I was the one person who went with me everywhere I went. I was interested, always curious for "the answer." I held many jobs and had many experiences. I went from one thing to another, always searching and never quite feeling like I belonged. I always felt different and I always felt like there was so much more to me if I could only find where I supposed to be so I could let it all out! When I was young, this feeling bothered me so I pushed it aside and hid it from others. I held myself back and kept things to myself because I thought there was something wrong or bad about my feeling this way or about my being different—if that was even true. (It occurred to me that this feeling may simply be an illusion. It's also possible that other people may feel this way too.) I didn't feel comfortable confiding in anyone and since no one else was talking about feeling different, again, I thought I was alone. Hence, I kept moving, taking job after job, still searching for answers outside myself, always wondering what this "life thing" was all about.

There were other things that changed for me as well during my twenties. I started to slowly believe in myself. I had experienced some achievements and some small successes. After my first degree, I decided to go into psychiatric nursing and pursued an associate and a bachelor's degree in nursing, graduating with honors. I have a passion for helping others unleash their greatness and at the time nursing seemed to be the best path. It turned out to be a perfect place to play—to learn my craft and develop my skills. I continued my formal education, receiving a master's in business administration.

I realized along my way that no one has all the answers to life's questions and the answers that seem to work for one person may not work for someone else. The reality is that each of us has to find our own path.

As I got older, I knew that I needed to find a way to let more of myself out. Over time I realized that I wasn't getting the answers from outside of me. I needed to find a way to accept myself as I am and to treat myself with greater respect and compassion. After all, life is a gift and it's up to me to figure out what I was meant to do with that gift. There is a reason for my existence at this time in history. I have a right to be here; I am no different than the trees, the stars, and the animals. I learned that I am okay—regardless of who I am—different or not. I was—and still am—determined to discover who I am and to become all that is possible for me in this lifetime.

Once I became okay with myself and once I knew that it was all right to be me—whatever I discovered to be true about myself—I gave myself permission to be me regardless of what others thought of me. At this moment, the world looked different to me and with this shift in perspective, I was different. I was bolder and more determined.

This book is the culmination of all of my searching. It's the journey that I uncovered to allow myself to be all there is of me. Oh, I'm hardly done; this book is just the start. This book provides you with the tools *you* need to discover and accept *yourself*, to be okay with who *you* are so you can live your best life. Once you have the tools to find your way, you continue to use them to learn and discover, grow and evolve, as a person. Each day is new and yet when you know how to be yourself, how to honor yourself, and how to be the best "you" you can be, then each day is a journey into authenticity.

You are a child of the universe. You are wonderful! And you deserve to have a great life. As you read through this book, you will learn how to know yourself, to accept what is, and then learn to make choices that honor your highest self. By reading this book, may you discover the art of wondering about you and may you find the peace, love, happiness, and fulfillment you desire all the days of your life journey.

Acknowledgments

Writing a book is a tremendous undertaking. Over a period of eighteen months, I spent countless hours working on this book, which in many ways is the completion of a chapter of my life. For the first twenty years of my adult life, I learned, asked questions, and sought answers. This book is the evidence of that inquiry.

It takes input from many different sources as well as the support of many people in order to accomplish this daunting task. To everyone who assisted me, I give thanks.

I want to thank my father, Harold Weiner, MD, for the multitude of lessons he taught me; without realizing it, he has been my greatest teacher. I am grateful for my mother, Bayle Weiner, for always standing by me. Like a rock, she is always there to listen, to encourage, and to dream for me. I am grateful for my sister and friend, Lori Weiner, for her unwavering support and love, and who helped show me where my greatness lies. I am also thankful for her editorial support and her incredible poem that she wrote after her first experience reading the manuscript. And I am thankful for Joshua, my son, who demonstrated extreme patience and understanding while I focused on completing this book. I am so grateful for his love and his presence in my life. He is truly a blessing.

Many thanks to my clients, without whom this book would not have been possible. They are my behind-the-scenes collaborators. The clarity would often come during coaching calls.

I want to acknowledge my friends who read the initial manuscript to determine whether the work made sense and who offered their commentary and suggestions for improvement: Nancy Baker, Cheryl Barrett, Sandy Cotteta, Linda Jeffries, and Patricia Washeleski. For their time and commitment, I am very grateful.

To my editor, Sue Collier, and to everyone at About Books, Inc., thank you so much for your incredible energy and support, and your unwavering standards of excellence.

I want to thank Cindy Diccianni, my business partner. She is truly a gift from the universe. The synergy that comes from our working together is incredible.

I want to express my gratitude to my ex-husband, John Richard Fuimano, who died in November 2002. His love made a huge impact in my life. By believing in me and holding that place of greatness for me to aspire to, he made it possible for me to gain the strength I needed to allow myself to fly.

Each of us has the power to transform the life of another. To all who have touched me in my life, I am grateful. And so I may touch you and make a difference in your life, this book is for you.

And finally, I am grateful to our Creator for the inspiration and guidance that brought this book to life.

May you experience peace, joy, and fulfillment all the days of your life.

Peace and love,

Julie Fuimano

Chapter One

Starting Your Journey

"To be what we are, and to become what we are capable of becoming, is the only end in life."
—Robert Louis Stevenson, poet, novelist, and essayist

Who am I? Why am I here? These questions have been pondered and explored by philosophers throughout the course of history. They've been debated and studied. In fact, in our own way, each of us must also answer these questions for ourselves.

So many of you are searching for your *own* answers. So many of you are working beneath *your* potential, knowing that there's more that's possible for you but perhaps not knowing *how* to find your path. So many of you are living unhappy lives—unhappy with your work, your kids, and your relationships not realizing that you have the power to change your situation. So many of you still ask the question, "What should I do when I grow up?" Not understanding that wherever you are on the continuum of life, you're simply still searching for yourself.

Perhaps you're asking the wrong questions. Perhaps instead of, "What should I do when I grow up?" the question you need to ask is, *"Who am I?"* and, *"Who do I want to be?"* The more you uncover and understand *who you are*, the more you understand life, and the easier it is to see what you're meant to do.

What you seek, what you long for, is to understand how to participate in this thing called "life." You want some assurances that you're doing it right, and you don't want to reach the end of your life realizing

1

that there was another—perhaps a better—way. You also want your life to mean something. You want to make some kind of difference while you're here. And you want to find happiness and personal fulfillment.

Happiness and personal fulfillment, as well as knowing you're living "right," cannot be found outside of you. It cannot be found in the eyes of someone else or in the possessions you accumulate. It cannot be found by comparing what you have to what someone else has. In fact, it cannot be found in external possessions. It can only be acknowledged *within* you. It's found in the day-to-day pleasures that you experience. It will be found on your deathbed when you can say, "I did it well." I don't know about you, but I think I'd rather gauge how I'm doing by how I feel on a day-to-day basis than wait until I'm on my deathbed!

No one knows what makes you happy except you. Everyone has different likes and dislikes and everyone finds happiness in different ways. The more you discover yourself and allow yourself to pursue what makes you happy, the more you maximize the results you achieve, the joy you experience, and the difference you make in the world.

The paradox of life is that for it to mean what you intend, for you to be fulfilled and happy with what you've made of your life, you need to take every moment seriously and eliminate the things that stand in your way by focusing on what you ultimately want to accomplish in your lifetime. And at the same time, keep it light, effortless, and learn how to play so you get the most enjoyment out of your time here. Sounds simple, doesn't it? Simple, yes; easy, no.

"Life is not holding a good hand; Life is playing a poor hand well."
—Danish proverb

Similar to a card game, in life you are dealt a hand that includes a body, a mind, parents, and perhaps some siblings as well as your socio-economic level, environment, culture, and geographic location—all of those things each of us starts out with that are unique to our situation.

Then, you learn how to play. You use your hand and make moves that bring you enjoyment. If a move causes you pain or suffering, you choose a different path. Or maybe you don't. Maybe you think that's just how the game is supposed to be played not realizing the power you hold in your ability *to choose*—to choose a different move or to play an entirely different game.

Whatever you learn through your childhood is supposed to prepare you to live as a responsible adult. But what does that mean? And does "responsible adult" include happiness and personal fulfillment?

That's what makes identity and personal fulfillment so challenging to discuss. After all, most people don't grow up learning to discover themselves; you're supposed to do that during your teenage years. You're taught to get a job so you can move out from your parents' home and pay your own way. But it's not like you wake up on your twentieth birthday with all the answers of who you are. The focus on creating a career, making money, and having a family has to include self-discovery and personal growth in order for you to experience the fulfillment you long for. Parents do the best they can while you are a child (which may or may not have been what you *wanted*) and then leave you to do the rest, which continues for as long as you live. You need to learn what it takes to feel comfortable in your own skin.

Focusing on your own personal development is the greatest gift you can give the world. By focusing your life on learning all there is to know about you, you not only discover the world within you but you also learn the awesome nature of life. The things that make you special and unique are waiting for you to discover and acknowledge so you can share them with the rest of us. And by cultivating your gifts and talents, you give yourself permission to focus on what is best about you, bringing you the most joy that is possible while giving the best of you to the world. By focusing on you, you shine your light on the world.

How do you go inside yourself? How do you travel within yourself, within your soul, to find the answers you seek? How do you find the courage to then make decisions based on your own personhood and not follow the predetermined paths that others will tell you are right for you? How do you learn to use your feelings to guide you toward your own sense of right and wrong and of happiness and fulfillment so you know you are living "right" *for you*? This book will show you how. *The Journey Called YOU* is a guide for traveling within, for understanding yourself and accepting yourself so you can make decisions every day that move you closer to the happy and fulfilled life you seek.

The journey itself is your life; the sooner you start your journey within, the sooner you can create the life you love. The goal of all life is to live it well, accomplish what you want, and make a difference so you know your life has meaning.

Your mission for playing along in *The Journey Called YOU* is to discover your gifts, develop them, experience them, share them with the world, eliminate anything that holds you back or stands in your way, and enjoy yourself along the way. You will learn how to use your personal power to free yourself to be *you*. You are the most important person in your life! Without you, what do you have?

There's nothing to fear in playing a game of self-discovery and acceptance. Be fearful of reaching the end of your life without really knowing yourself and the possibilities of all you could've been if you'd have seen and explored more of *you*.

There are people who enjoy living mediocre lives. These are the people who fear life—and by not truly living, they fear death. These people will try to hold you back, not wanting you to break free to experience all that's possible for you, out of fear and out of the sheer desire to maintain the status quo. Throughout this book, you will learn how to create boundaries to protect you from these naysayers and how to overcome your fears of greatness.

Yes, greatness. You possess greatness—we each do. It is your job—your life's purpose—to discover your greatness and share it with the world.

There are others who are not on the same evolutionary path as you are. You need to know that where you are is perfect and where they are is perfect. You experience much less stress if you stop judging others and yourself, stop wishing things were different, and accept people as they are. You cannot change anyone else. The only person you can change is you.

When you focus on *you*, you actually raise the bar for others. By learning to overcome the obstacles that are in your path, you can teach others to do the same. By no longer tolerating people or things that get in the way of your experiencing happiness and joy and by learning to challenge the rules set by others and create your own rules, you set a higher standard for you and for people interested in spending time with you. As you learn this path for yourself, you become a role model for others.

It starts by giving yourself permission—permission to experience joy every day, permission to feel good all the time, permission to do just those things that you enjoy, permission to let go of struggle, permission to eliminate the obstacles that stand in the way of success, permission to be successful and enjoy your success. It means you'll need to keep an open mind and recognize that in order to get different results in your life, you need to start doing things differently. Be open to the exercises in this book. Be open to explore yourself.

The fact is that by *not* knowing yourself, by keeping yourself hidden, you are actually more vulnerable to hurt and pain. It's when we deny the things we need the most—to understand and acknowledge our feelings, to be who we are—that we become vulnerable to personal attacks from others and to stress. When you accept everything there is to know about you, nothing and no one can hurt you. When you learn to use your body and emotions to determine what is best for you and you base your decisions on your intuition and on honoring your integrity, you transcend vulnerability and become almost invincible as you open yourself up to be authentic, pure, and genuine. Your feelings and emotional energy become the guides for your behavior, and you learn to respond in ways that honor you and others around you.

The tools in this book present a way of wondering about yourself. It's wonder with a purpose. And it's not just for you to play but also for you to play with others including your employees, your children, and your spouse—to help them to learn more about themselves. It's a game of self-discovery and self-acceptance.

Self-discovery is not a chore; it's a game. It is fun and exciting. It's a game of wonder! And if you play the game, you're always a winner. You only lose when you choose not to play. You know people who aren't interested in learning more about themselves. These are the people who are blind to how they impact others around them. They come in like a tornado, leaving destruction in their wake. People who choose not to play, who are not open to discovering and improving themselves, hurt not only themselves but do the world a disservice too, because we will not benefit from seeing and experiencing the best of them. If you have someone like this in your life, remember, you cannot change him or her; you can only change who you are with this person. You can learn how to be the best you can be in spite of this person's level of personal development. In fact, people like this are often your greatest teachers, causing you to stretch yourself to communicate more effectively, ask directly for what you need, set limits on the behaviors tolerated by others, and spend time with people who are more interested in developing themselves.

Through the book you will learn methods to get to know yourself at a deeper level and to accept the person that you are. It's not about boasting; it is about uncovering the greatness that is within you and letting it shine through. It's about being who you are already and who you have the capacity to become. The fact is that you already *are* wonderful. Don't you want to discover *how* you are wonderful and *all* that's possible for you to become?

Boasting is a way for people to feel good about themselves. This behavior implies that they don't feel good about who they are and therefore seek validation from others. Boasting usually occurs when someone puffs him- or herself up at the expense of someone else. People who are comfortable with who they are have no need for boasting. They speak from a different place—humble, yet confident.

Discovering *who you are* is a process that requires an investment of time, energy, and openness. It also requires a commitment to become nonjudgmental and compassionate with *you*. It requires you to think differently so you learn to behave differently.

So, *who are you?* And how do you get started? First, you need to understand what constitutes the "who." What does it mean when I ask you to discover "who" you are? And how can you learn to consider the "who" in your daily activities?

In Chapter Two, you will learn what I mean when I refer to the "who." Rarely are the conversations you have with people focused on discovering and developing yourself. You need to learn how to venture into this territory. Discussions about *who you are* sound different and have a different impact from what people usually focus on. In order to begin *The Journey Called YOU*, you must know how to access this deeper level.

Chapter Three describes the self-discovery process and starts you on your way to exploring you and your nature.

In Chapter Four, you learn to break free of the rules and the conditioned behavior you learned when you were young. Separating from the rules you were taught and that developed your early belief systems is necessary for you to set yourself free to live your life in the way that brings you the most joy.

Chapter Five guides you through identifying and establishing your own vision for success. Afterward, you will read through a personal story from "The Journey Called ME" that helps to integrate some of the learning that's taken place so far.

In Chapter Six, you are introduced to the Time Enjoyment Model™ so you can learn to use your time in the way that maximizes who you are.

Chapter Seven teaches you what you need to know to live every day in a way that honors the best of who you are in order to maximize the life you create on your journey. By learning to honor the wonderful person you are and living in integrity, you establish new rules for living a life that works for you.

In the final chapter, Chapter Eight, you'll learn what it's like to live "The Journey." There are several quotes from clients in this chapter who have evolved through coaching to the point where they are beginning to live their own "Journey."

All client comments, stories, and names have been modified for use in the book.

To get the most from reading this book, I recommend you keep a journal so you can write your responses to the questions posed, do the exercises at the end of each chapter, and address anything that might come up for you as you read through the book. Focus your journaling on what you experience—any emotions, thoughts, or ideas that come up as you read or the identification with any of the obstacles presented throughout the book. A journal is a safe place for you to explore and express your inner world.

Please keep an open mind as you read through the book. There may be lots of learning that takes place for you, so go at your own pace. This is not like reading a novel; you may need to read this book in bits and pieces. Set aside some quiet time each day to read a bit and process what you've read. When you've completed the book, go back and read it through again for more thorough learning. Your experience will be different the second time around. This is not easy material to master. Give yourself time to master living *The Journey Called YOU*. The good news is that your journey lasts a lifetime.

There are many obstacles we each face as a part of life. These obstacles are often referred to by my coaching clients as "clouds" that obstruct the path or hold you back from where you want to go. Obstacles are not walls; they're like fog making it difficult to see your way clear, meaning you just need a guide to lead you through this mist. For this reason, the obstacles presented throughout the book are introduced as "A Walk Through the Clouds." Each "walk" you take not only identifies the obstacle but provides you with the tools needed to move beyond the impact of the obstacle so you can make your way clear of the cloud. You have the power to walk through these clouds; I will teach you how to access that power. Clouds are distracting because you focus on the obstacle rather than what's beyond. Living in the midst of clouds is draining and time-consuming. Together, we'll move through the clouds so you can see your way clear to create the fulfillment and peace you desire for your life journey.

At the end of each chapter, you'll find a coaching challenge offering several questions for you to ponder. Use your journal to consider your answers to these questions and enjoy the inquiry. As your coach for *The Journey Called YOU*, I am your partner. Feel free to contact me with questions, comments, or simply to share your revelations. I'd love to hear from you. Email me at Julie@NurturingYourSuccess.com.

"If I am not for myself, who will be for me? If I am only for myself, what am I? If not now, when?"
—[Rabbi] Hillel

Chapter Two

Getting to the "Who"

"This is your life. Right here. Right now. Just this. Your life is your very own path. Don't wish for someone else's; instead search for ways to be like your own true self and fulfill all your own promise and possibility. You are the spiritual treasure you are trying to discover and reveal."
—Lama Surya Das, author of *Awakening the Buddhist Heart*

Your goal in life is to fully discover who you are and to develop yourself as a person.

You are complete and whole. You have everything you need to become the person you were meant to be. Through self-discovery and acceptance, you open the door to achieving greater potential. This potential exists inside you, waiting for you to let it out. As you come to know yourself, you begin to express confidence in being who you are. You naturally give yourself permission to be you. You learn to honor and respect yourself. You express yourself more clearly and confidently. And just like a flower in springtime, you bloom.

Before we start the self-discovery process, we need to understand what we mean by "who." When we talk about "who" you are, what am I asking you to discover? How do we access and talk about the "who"? This is not an easy question to answer. We are asking "who," not "what," "why," or "how," and yet we need to look at these questions so we can better understand how to access the "who." This understanding is essential to your journey, so bear with me through this chapter. I promise it will all come together in the end. Be patient. After reading the book in its entirety, reread this chapter and you'll see how much you've learned.

What

> "When a day passes, it is no longer there. What remains of it? Nothing more than a story...Today we live, but tomorrow today will be a story. The whole world, all human life, is one long story...To the storyteller yesterday is still here."
>
> —I. B. Singer, the Yiddish Literature Nobel Prize laureate

When someone says to you, "Tell me about yourself," how do you reply? If you're like most people, you reply with what you do for a living—a nurse, a doctor, a lawyer, an executive, a manager, a bank teller. You describe the roles you play in life, such as husband or wife, father or mother, grandfather or grandmother, and you tell people all about your children and grandchildren. You may describe some of the things you enjoy doing such as gardening, skiing, artistry, golfing, or bike riding.

But you are not your roles or your hobbies. *Who you are* is not what you do for a living. Your job is a merely a means for expressing *who you are*.

In fact, most conversations focus on *things*. People talk about the news, politics, their job, management, their schedule, sports, the weather, what's for dinner, and so on. On a day-to-day basis, stories are told to tell us what's happening and to keep us informed. There are stories about work and what happened with the kids and who did what to whom. It's easy to get lost in these areas because this is what people talk about and it's both important and meaningful to have these conversations. These conversations focus on what I call the "what" of life.

People don't know how to talk about themselves. They don't really know how to get to know *who* they are. It's so difficult to put a handle on the "who" stuff and articulate what you really mean to say that you settle for talking about all the other stuff—*the story*.

People love stories! We read newspaper stories about things people have done. We read stories in books of people's lives, the voyages they take, and the missions they've accomplished. People use stories throughout history. There are fables and myths; even the bible tells stories. By reading the story, we learn we're not alone, that others have the same struggles and triumphs. We learn new approaches, perspectives, and possibilities. Stories whisk us away to another time and place. And in every story, there are lessons to be learned.

Through stories you learn different ways in which lessons present themselves. Stories provide us with more than just what happened. They provide examples to make a point or convey an idea. Stories help to give the lesson context, making it easy to remember the lesson; they give people something to tie the message to. And you'll remember how the story made you feel. Stories are wonderful ways for us to connect with and understand others.

In fact, years ago storytelling was a way of life. Stories would be told and retold, passed down from generation to generation. In the days before radio and television, people used stories as a way to connect and for entertainment. Children would sit around elders, who would tell stories about life, love, events, situations, and lessons. Today, however, people do not connect in this way. Our elders are not the center of attention in our society. They are often kept separated from the mainstream, and their usefulness is not capitalized. The integration of elders within the community is imperative for us to thrive as a population. There is so much wisdom in the stories; and we have so much to learn.

There is a place for stories in our lives. What's important is that we recognize that it is, in fact, just a story. You are not your stories.

It's easy to get caught up in the story of the day. Some people simply enjoy the drama of the story. Others tell you their story to try to evoke in you the same feeling that they are experiencing. They want to feel okay for experiencing that feeling. They want to know that whatever they are feeling is okay and the only way most people know how to get that validation is to get you to experience it with them. It's easier to tell you the story than to talk about the feelings directly. People focus their energy on the story, in hopes that others will understand what they really want to communicate.

Having spent many years in healthcare, I have lots of stories to tell. Healthcare is one of those industries where the stories are so fantastic, you are easily captivated and mesmerized by the details. I've had healthcare clients who would recite stories of the day to me and I've stopped them to ask questions. I wanted to know how they felt and

what they thought about the event or what they learned about themselves in experiencing this incident. This was different for them because
they were not accustomed to anyone asking about *them* personally. Most
people just want to hear the story. People easily get so wrapped up in
hearing *what* happened that they don't realize that the person telling
the story has a reason for telling it; there's something here they need to
identify about themselves, their feelings, and their fears, or perhaps
they wouldn't be sharing the story.

Yes, there are some people who simply enjoy telling stories and
there are others who hide in storytelling and still others who long for
someone to guide them *in* so they can understand their feelings associated with this story. They tell the story hoping to come to some sort of
understanding that doesn't seem to come. After all, it's just a story.
Knowing *what* happened isn't enough. The answers to life's questions
lie *beneath* the story.

When you're trying to understand life and come to terms with what
the universe has given you and what it wants of you, living in the story
won't give you the answers you seek. The story itself isn't what's important; it's what you learn from the story—what you learn about others,
yourself, and life itself.

It's easy to get caught up in the story or the drama mistakenly thinking that it *is* life. But it's not. A story is just a story. Each of us will have
to endure loss and pain, pleasure and joy. Everyone has his or her own
story to tell. And although a story may be fascinating, it's what people
learn from their stories and what they do with that knowledge and
understanding that matters. It's not the story, you see, but the *experience* of the story and the people who share our story with us—who cry
with us, laugh with us, live with us, love with us. That's where true
fortune lies and that's what makes life grand.

When I mentioned earlier that I had used drugs when I was younger,
I neglected to share the *story* of that time of my life. I did not tell you
the details of what I did, what happened to me, all that I went through,
or how that impacted my family. That's the story of my youth. Simply
stating that it happened is enough to make my point. Had I told you
the story, the point would have been lost amid the drama of the story.
What's important is what I learned, and how I am able to use the experience and the lessons from that time of my life to make a better life for
myself and to make a difference in the lives of others.

If you think about the story, it's what happened to me and what I did. But consider what the story tells you about "who" I was at the time. Clearly, people who use drugs are lost. They are hiding from life or from something painful. They cannot face themselves or their feelings. They do not love themselves and cannot accept themselves. This was me some twenty years ago. That was *who I was*; that's not who I am today. But going through those experiences allowed me the opportunity to discover myself; unfortunately, I had to make life really, really bad until I could wake up to the reality of what life was truly about. I had to hit rock bottom before I could start to make decisions about who I wanted to be.

With each event, mistake, or situation you find yourself in, there are several elements: what happened, the meaning you assign to it, how you feel about it, and what you choose to do about it. What happened isn't nearly as important as what you do with it. The meaning you assign to the event impacts your life in ways that you may not realize. Events happen; there is no meaning other than what you assign to it and usually, that meaning clouds your way.

You can lose yourself in the story—in the "what"—rather than deal with the feelings in the moment (your feelings are more about "who" you are and we'll discuss this in detail in a later chapter). In fact, people do many things to avoid or deny their feelings including acting out behavior, addictions, overeating, even gossip, and other self-indulgent activities.

When people look for validation and understanding, they long to connect with themselves at a deeper level. They want to understand *who* they are, how they think and feel about things. They want to understand why they believe things the way they do and what drives them to make certain choices. They want to know why they aren't achieving the results they want or why they cannot find the right job or the right mate. Since few people are trained to help you understand yourself, it's a challenging and lonely road to gain that understanding.

But it doesn't have to be lonely, and there is a road to follow. The journey moves you from living in the "what" of life to discovering "who" you are. In fact, it is often the "what" that opens the door to discovering who you are. The story can be used as a way into the "who."

For example, I met Susan at the nail salon. We were drying our nails when we started talking about the holidays. She told me she was having her family over for a holiday dinner—forty people. She had this dinner every year at her home; none of her siblings took turns, and although they did bring dessert, that was all the support she received. She didn't sound excited about this, so I asked, "What would your ideal holiday dinner look like?"

She replied, "Just the seven of us: my husband, my kids, my mother, and me."

"So, what stops you?" I asked.

She told me that she's been having this dinner every year since her mother was no longer able. None of the siblings had ever offered and "I have the biggest house anyway."

Through the conversation, it became clear that she never thought to question the tradition. She did what she did because this was the way it was done. And over the years, the family just grew. Her siblings married and had kids. She never stopped to consider how she felt about it; she never considered doing something different. This is her story.

Susan was surprised when I suggested she let everyone know that next year she won't be making dinner for the entire family. Instead, she could create her ideal holiday dinner. Honestly, perhaps the other members of the family would like to do other things as well. She replied, "You mean I can do that? Just tell everyone I'm not doing it anymore?"

"Are you asking me if you have permission to do what makes you happy?" I asked. "The permission to live in the way that makes you the happiest exists within you. You must give it to yourself."

I wondered how these behaviors affected other areas of her life. What else was she putting up with simply because she never stopped to consider whether she was enjoying herself? How much of her identity is wrapped up in what others think of her? How much of her life is focused on pleasing others? What else is she doing out of habit rather than out of the sheer joy of it? Questions also come up for me about her ability to delegate and set limits, and how these might be impeding her path to happiness. How does it serve her or limit her to put the needs of others before her own?

By being curious about Susan and asking her additional questions, we could help her to see herself and her motivations more clearly. In this way, we could have a conversation with her that would provide meaning, and support her to make decisions about what she wants so she can start to create a life, in addition to a holiday dinner, that supports her and honors what she believes to be ideal for her. By having a conversation that extends a bit deeper than just the story, we can assist her in exploring who she is, identifying the obstacles in her way, and discovering what makes her happy. The conversation could focus on increasing her awareness and empowering her to make choices that bring her joy. It's easy to make better decisions when you are more aware of the dynamics under which you live.

Our conversation didn't last long enough for me to ask too many more questions, but I know that I started her thinking differently that day.

This kind of conversation looks and feels very different from one merely discussing the menu for the dinner, complaining about all that has to be done, or sharing the misery by talking about what you're dreading about the holidays.

There are several different questions to ask when going from the story to the "who." When a situation occurs, you can learn to discover the person behind the story—whether that person is you or someone else. Storytelling enables us to get closer to *who the person is* by asking some simple questions without getting stuck in the story itself.

- How do you feel about the event/situation/person?
- What is meaningful to you about this?
- What does this story mean in the course of your life?
- How does that relate to your life today?
- What do you want to have happen?
- What does this story tell you about *you?* What does it say about the other person?
- What can you learn from the story or from your reaction to the story?

When you journal about an event, use these questions to guide you rather than simply focusing on the details of the story.

The story itself can be distracting. The story is the shield that keeps you from *you*—from your *Truth*. It's not strength to hold onto the story; that only keeps you in pain and keeps you struggling for answers.

The story is what happened, the situation, or the people. It's about the past, not the present. It's what you've seen or experienced or done. Living in the past will make the present go away.

Stories can also be about the future. Planning the future is fun. But there are those people who lose themselves in making plans, discussing expectations, or fantasizing. This distracts from the reality of the present moment and does not allow the person to be fully who they are. People can also become anxious and worrisome about the future. This takes the person out of the present and places him or her in a world of fantasy. People waste precious life moments worrying about things that never come to pass. It's the "what-if" game and it gets you nowhere. There is no joy in playing this game. If you find yourself playing what-if scenarios in your head, stop, breathe, and focus on what you know to be true in the current moment. This moment is the only thing that is real.

The fact is, most people spend their time discussing either the past or the future. The present is where the richness of life exists. The memories you have that are the most vivid for you will be the ones where you remember how you felt, what it looked like, what you heard, smelled, and tasted. When your senses are completely engrossed in whatever you are doing and you are completely aware, you are experiencing the moment. With so many distractions, it's challenging to remain fully engaged in the present for periods of time. Noticing when you are stuck in the story is one way to pull yourself back into the present.

Barbara was a client who was struggling with a relationship with her sister. They were entering the same line of business. Barbara was excited and looking forward to achieving much success; her sister was treating it more like a hobby. Barbara started sharing with me the dynamics between the two of them, how her sister treated her, how her sister acted like their mother, what it was like when they were growing up. This was the story of their relationship.

None of that matters in the present. What matters is how she wants to be treated today and how she wants the relationship to be between the two of them. How does she want to feel in this relationship? What does she want the relationship to mean in her life today? The story of their past doesn't matter because at this moment Barbara can redefine the relationship between the two of them and then ask for what she wants and needs from her. She needs to focus her attention on what success looks like in her new business venture, regardless of what her sister does, and not allow herself to be distracted by the drama of the story between the two of them.

A Walk Through the Clouds: Minimizing

Sometimes you don't get lost in the story, but you don't recognize the significance of it. Minimizing is when you tell yourself that it's not that bad; you belittle the issue, the story, or your feelings about the story. You may do this because you don't want to make a big deal of it.

Making less of a situation is not helpful. It does not acknowledge the full impact nor does it allow you to acknowledge your feelings about it. Often people minimize because they are not sure how to handle their feelings or the situation itself.

When you discover you are minimizing, this often signals to you that you need to take a closer look. There is something here for you to look at and learn from.

Until you recognize the situation for what it is, the lesson will repeat itself until you are ready and/or willing to view the whole issue for what it really is.

Dawn was a coaching client who minimized her feelings about relationships with others. She initiated the contact with me to assist her in changing careers. The first thing that came up was her unhappiness in her marriage. As Dawn started divorce proceedings, it became evident that she was avoiding dealing with her feelings regarding her husband. The things she talked about supported their incompatibility, so I suggested she spend some time considering the factors that went into choosing him as her mate.

Dawn realized she had a pattern of minimizing her feelings with regard to relationships with others. She was able to identify others in her life, a friend in particular, who had hurt her badly. And yet she minimized the situation in which this person hurt her; she even took responsibility for the situation and blamed herself. By doing this, she was telling herself that her feelings didn't matter. By not acknowledging her feelings, Dawn denied her Inner Self the proper amount of recognition and support. Her self-esteem suffered. She gave the event lesser meaning than it deserved and until she was ready to deal with it fully, her behaviors would continue to haunt her relationships.

Dawn needed to learn to acknowledge her feelings when things didn't seem right. Then she could stand up for herself and let the other person know what was bothering her so they could learn how she wanted to be treated. The other person may not realize he or she is doing anything wrong unless Dawn lets him or her know about it. In this way, she honors both herself and others.

Rationalizing and making excuses are two ways in which people minimize situations or their feelings. It's human nature to rationalize. We are rational beings, after all. It's important that you appreciate when you are rationalizing so you are fully aware of what you are doing.

People make excuses to justify their behavior or the situation. If you are going to apologize for something, just apologize. When you start to make excuses, it signifies that you haven't accepted responsibility; you're still trying to justify your actions. The excuses minimize the impact and the meaning of the apology, making it insincere. When you accept responsibility, there are no excuses. You made a mistake. Now you know it, you've acknowledged it, and you can move on. We all make mistakes. Welcome to *Club Human*.

The word "but" usually signifies an excuse. Everything that comes after the "but" is an excuse, negating the message that preceded it. Be careful how you use this word. Realize that when you give feedback to someone, whether it's a coworker, friend, or child, and you use the word "but," people have difficulty receiving the message. They become defensive. If you compliment someone or say something positive, and then use the word "but," you cancel out the positive part of your message. Use "and" in place of "but." When you use "and," you honor the positive part of the message, you can give the feedback you desire, and the other person will be open to hear your whole message.

COACHING TIP: The way to eliminate minimizing is to recognize how the event, situation, or person has affected you. Give it the proper amount of attention. Make a big deal of it! Whatever it is, deal with it completely. Do not minimize any situation—good or bad. In fact, labeling an event "good" or "bad" assigns meaning to it. The event is what it is, neither good nor bad. Learn the lessons that exist in every situation and celebrate your learning.

Stop communicating with yourself in a way that does not honor your highest self. Minimizing yourself is never helpful and serves absolutely no purpose other than to diminish your self-esteem and delay learning the lesson. Allow your Inner Self to experience the range of emotions that come up for you. In this way, you honor your body as it communicates to you. Only by learning to experience the full range of emotions brought about by the event or circumstance can you move through and beyond it. That's how you evolve.

Learn to recognize when you are making excuses or rationalizing your behavior. Accept responsibility for yourself. Do not minimize the impact of your mistake by minimizing the effect it had on others. It is what it is. By accepting full responsibility for your own actions and apologizing simply, you demonstrate sincerity and can move beyond the situation.

Why

The question "why" is the search for reasons. There are times when understanding why you do things is helpful, like when you find yourself stuck in an unfulfilling place in your life or when you notice patterns in your life. "Why" is also helpful when you are instituting a change in your life.

Karen was leaving her husband after many years of marriage. She knew "why" she was leaving; she was freeing herself to be who she wanted to be and live how she wanted to live. The marriage had been fraught with distrust, and she felt as though she lived in a prison, always being berated with questions, unable to live peacefully and in ways that brought her joy or that allowed her to express her true nature. By holding in her heart and in her mind the reasons why she was leaving and what made the marriage unbearable, as well as holding onto the vision she has for a great life, she was able to take the necessary steps to honor herself.

If you choose to use the question "why," be careful not to get trapped by the desire to figure it all out. It can be distracting, taking you away from focusing on the things you want to accomplish. The fact is that you may not be able to answer that question. The answer may reveal itself at some point on your journey or it may not. What's most important is that you get to know who you are, that you learn to make decisions based on what you want, and make choices that support your quest for a fulfilling life.

Consider a time when you watched a news story unfold on television. They present the facts as they know them and then they spend hours—even days—talking about the event from every possible angle. The analysis is fun and it certainly brings the television station high ratings, but it's time-consuming and doesn't get you to the answer. It usually just brings up more questions. The answer won't be known until all of the facts are in. Unless you enjoy the analysis, which many people do, there are other ways to spend your time and energy.

People spend their entire lives trying to come up with some of the "why" questions—and answers—to life. It's a fun place to play. But when it comes to self-discovery, it can hinder or help.

"Why" can make you wish you had done things differently. It can make you feel sorry for yourself and regret all the things you didn't do when you had the chance. It can bring feelings of inadequacy and self-pity. "Why" can make you crazy!

Therapists and psychologists live in the "why." They help you to understand why you do the things you do and how you got to where you are. They look at past events and journey with you into your childhood years to help you understand yourself better and to determine what might be blocking you from moving forward in your life.

Psychiatrists diagnose mental disorders and treat mental illness through the use of medication and other methods. Their role for the most part is to help you regain a certain level of mental functioning so you can process and think more clearly.

These professionals are critical if you are unable to accept yourself and love yourself. If you experience some block as you go through this book, find a professional to discuss your thoughts and feelings. Part of playing this game of self-exploration is to take complete responsibility for yourself and your enjoyment in life. If there is something unfinished or if you find yourself stuck and unable to break through, do what you have to in order to free yourself.

Although there's a place for analysis, you can become paralyzed by it. It's like a spiral that keeps you going around and around in circles without forward movement. Knowing "why" won't be what moves you forward. Answering "why," even if you can, doesn't change the facts of what occurred and asking "why" won't put you into action. Asking "why" is an intellectually stimulating activity. And although it may be fun, it doesn't bring you to that feeling place where your soul lives. Ultimately, it doesn't matter why. What matters is what you choose to do *regardless* of why.

Asking "why" might lead you to look for scapegoats, people to blame for your lot in life. Often the people you blame are your parents; after all, they're easy targets. Parents do the best job they know how, given their own upbringing, education, and personal development. They teach you what they can and at some point it's up to you to accept responsibility for your life. It was their job to start you on your path and give you direction. At some point, you must take the lead and chart your own course, answer your own questions, and make your own rules.

Whether you *liked* how your parents raised you or whether you *agree* with their choices is something else; it's called judgment. The fact is that it doesn't matter whether you liked how they raised you, unless you want to use the knowledge to learn how to raise your own children. Whether you got the parenting you wanted or not, you got what you got. The experiences you had offered you opportunities to learn certain lessons; that's what you're here to do—experience life, learn lessons, and share those lessons with others. Let go of the belief that childhood is supposed to be a certain way. It is what it is and it's a unique experience for each of us.

In many cultures, people believe that before you are born you choose your parents. This choice is based on who you believe will give you the best chance at accomplishing what you are meant to do during this lifetime.

What this means is that you take a wider view of your life, look at what it means in the course of history over time, rather than just one twenty-four-hour period. When you look at your life from a larger perspective and consider your connection to the universe, it's easy to see how we are all connected and how, perhaps, you fit into the scheme of things. There are things you are meant to learn and things you are meant to teach. Your presence alone has an impact on anyone with whom you come in contact. There is a bigger vision and purpose here, even if we don't know it or understand it.

To ask "why" your parents were the way they were is not helpful; they did what they did because it's what they knew. That's all there is to know. Most parents don't intentionally do their children harm. They just don't know to do things differently. What matters is that you figure out a way to move beyond blaming your parents, beyond the anger and disappointment, and pick up where they left off. If you move from blaming and harboring anger at what your parents didn't do or didn't do well to a place of gratitude for what you've been able to become in spite of who they are, what would that be like?

Dana is a client who struggled with anger toward her mother for how she was brought up. Her father died when she was young and her mother was mentally impaired. Growing up, Dana was ashamed of her mom. And while other kids were outside playing, Dana was holding down a job so she could have money to buy clothes and other items she needed to survive.

Dana was burdened by this. Her anger fueled her through the years; it kept her distanced from her husband because she carried with her a shield of protection. Although clearly this cloud needed to be overcome, Dana was extremely successful. She was very bright. She had put herself through college, paying her tuition in cash along the way. She purchased her own home and started two businesses, selling the first for a profit. I met Dana at a networking function and she hired me because she was ready to do something else with her life but wasn't sure what that was. At our first session, she brought up the anger she held regarding her mother.

Through our work, Dana was able to see how her mother taught her quite well, even if it was by default. Dana had used her own desire to motivate her to succeed. Yes, she learned to protect herself first and foremost, which often kept people out or at a distance. But the anger she held made her act in certain beneficial ways that fueled her to achieve the successes she experienced up until this point in her life. She needed to confront the cloud of her mother and make some choices about how she wanted her mother to affect her life today. When Dana realizes that she no longer has to live under the cloud of who her mother was, but moves into acceptance of her life as it is today, she will liberate herself to continue to choose pleasure over pain. By continuing to harbor ill feelings about life growing up with her mother, she remains in pain. By letting go and accepting what happened—her story—as being the perfect playground for her to develop and grow to become the flower she is today, she allows herself to bloom. This means Dana needs to give up the story. She can no longer be attached to the story, or her anger. This way of thinking takes time and a personal commitment to move beyond the anger and into a place of acceptance and self-love. You cannot hold onto anger and practice self-love. It doesn't work.

Once Dana removes her anger and gives up the story related to her mother and how she raised her, there will be additional work for her to do. Dana will need to identify how the "shield of protection" has shaped her life. She will no longer need this shield, which means that other things in her life might change.

Make a decision today to come to terms with your parents so you feel good about creating a great life for you. Give yourself permission to leave your past behind you. Journal about each of your parents with the intention of coming to terms with them, finding acceptance of the people they are. You cannot change them, nor can you change what came before. Focus on what you can control: You and the choices you make about how to live in the present, and how you allow your parents and the things from your past to affect your life today. You have the power to do and to think differently.

A Walk Through the Clouds: The Blame Game

The Blame Game is when you focus your attention on blaming someone or something for the problem or situation. This wastes precious time and energy and accomplishes nothing except making another person feel bad and taking the focus off the problem. Blaming creates an environment of fear. Everyone makes mistakes; it's part of being human.

The fact is that it rarely matters who did it. What matters is what happened, why it happened (if that's possible to determine), what can be done to fix it, and what can be learned from it. It only matters "who" if there are training or teaching issues. If you identify "what" and "why" rather than "who-done-it," you can use the situation as an opportunity to learn and grow. When you respond to events as opportunities, you move forward faster. Ask yourself what responsibility *you* have in this situation? How are *you* getting in the way? What can *you* do differently or how do you need to be different in order to bring about different results? Always look for ways that you may be responsible or may have contributed. What are you putting up with? Focus on *you*; that way you can see how you can improve or change so you can move forward.

— — — — — — — — —

COACHING TIP: Focus on defining the problem, identifying the source of the problem, and crafting possible solutions. Then you can focus on correcting the situation, learning your lessons, and ensuring it doesn't recur. Blaming points the finger at others, at things, people, or situations outside you. It's the art of seeking external forces to shoulder the responsibility for the things that occur in your life. You become a victim of circumstance.

When you accept responsibility for everything that occurs in your life, you can then focus on determining what you are doing to bring about these outcomes. What is attracting this to you at this time? You have a lot more power than you realize. When you seek to place blame, you actually give your power away! When you accept responsibility, you may not like the situation you find yourself in, but what it means is that you got yourself here through the choices you've made up until this point. This means that you can learn to make different choices and create something new. You have the power.

When you blame others, it means you have not yet accepted responsibility for your life. No one else will. If you are unhappy with the results, then it's up to you to do something about it.

One of the hardest things for people to accept is that people are who they are and they make their own choices. The person does not change unless there is a great impetus *from within* to do so. Many people cause themselves stress over trying to get another person to act as they want them to act or to be. You don't have control over another person! Wondering "why" people do the things they do is a fruitless exercise.

People seeking self-understanding thrive on self-discovery and change. They look for it. They crave it. The status quo is not good enough and so we are always in search of better ways to think, to do things, and to expand the possibilities. On the other hand, there are many people who enjoy the way things are and seek to maintain the status quo. It's comfortable.

But comfortable breeds complacency. And if you find yourself comfortable with something, it's important to note whether you are actually enjoying it or whether it is a "familiar" kind of comfortable. People stay too long in situations that are uncomfortably familiar, torturing themselves simply because they're used to it or perhaps it takes too much energy to do something different. Or perhaps they don't know how, or they fear what life would be like if things were different. This might be a good time to ask yourself "why": Why *do* you stay in a relationship that is unhealthy and unhappy? Why do you stay in a job that brings you no satisfaction, where there's no room for growth or promotion, where you're not being challenged or stretched to your capacity, and where you're not making enough money?

Even if you know why, it won't move you to do something about it without the desire to have things be different and the willingness to do something about it. Some better questions might be, "Is this what you really want? How does it serve you to continue on this way? What are you gaining? What *do* you really want?"

Sometimes "why" will make you stop and take note of your life and where you are headed or whether you are off track. Refrain from spending so much time on the "why." In particular, do not get caught up in the "why me." Rather, use "why" as an impetus for understanding and moving forward. If you cannot figure out why you stay in an unfulfilling marriage, job, or situation, then envision what life would be if you were fulfilled. What would it take for life to be enjoyable?

A Walk Through the Clouds: The "Why Me" Trap

Self-pity has no value. Things happen. They happen to all of us. We each have a story to tell. There are lessons we all must learn. These lessons are not personal. Each of us must experience our share of loss and pain; it's part of our human experience. We mustn't be attached to any of it. Each of us must learn to deal with hardship and unpleasant feelings, as well as joy and pleasant feelings. Suffering is a choice and pity gets you nowhere.

COACHING TIP: Understand that sometimes things happen that are not the way you want them to be. And it feels bad. But be assured that things are unfolding as they should. Trust that whatever happens is for the good, even if you can't see it or understand it at the time.

Freeing yourself to be *you* starts with giving yourself permission. And while it sounds simple, some people find it challenging. You may have received messages in your childhood that convinced you that you are not all right, that you are not able to do anything without another person's approval, or that you are not good enough or worthy to have a great life.

Whatever the message, if you continue to harbor it, then it is running your life. A belief was formed and you live your life based on this limiting belief. Your beliefs or thoughts lead to your actions, which cause the results in your life. If you live your life based on a set of rules programmed in your brain by someone else, then your happiness will be limited. These rules create a ceiling for your success and hold you back from enjoying yourself and creating a great life.

As an adult, you have the power to make better choices. These beliefs that have created a barrier to your success need to be challenged and adjusted. You can choose to see a therapist, psychologist, or counselor, or you can just decide to adopt new beliefs—whatever works for you. You can also choose to work with a professional coach and simply create what you want in your life, regardless of what came before.

Tread lightly with the reason behind the things you do. Instead of "why," ask yourself, "How does this serve me?" Your response to that question will lead the way to self-discovery and will help you make choices about where to go from here.

Your goal in the self-discovery game is to take an inventory of who you are today, not who you were at some other point in your life or even how you came to be the way you are. Sometimes you discover "why" you are the way you are just by putting the question out to the universe and doing the other discovery work. There's much less stress and struggle when you choose to not focus too much energy on "why," but rather focus on creating what you want in spite of the reasons for how you got to this place.

How

"How" is another wonderful question. There are literally thousands of how-to books that give instructions on how to accomplish something or complete a task. People attend colleges and classes to learn how to do stuff. It's a wonderful place to play.

Not knowing how to accomplish something can keep you stuck. But often the issue is not that you don't know how, it might be that you are not yet committed to taking the necessary actions to change things or that you're not yet ready to give up your commitment to the way things are.

COACHING NOTE: Understanding Commitment

You are committed to something. Either you are committed to keeping things the way things are or you are committed to change. If there is some area of your life where you find yourself going in circles and not progressing, ask yourself, "What am I committed to?" By understanding your commitment, you learn what is driving your actions. Then you can accept that this is where you are right now in your life. And you can make a choice about what you want to be committed to as you create a life that brings you more joy.

"How" involves the discussions around strategy and planning. You discuss "how" you'll accomplish all of your errands or "how" you'll prepare your next project. You'll plan for your vacations and what you'll do on your days off.

People spend a lot of time and energy planning things. Strategic planning is fun. But if you plan too far in advance without flexibility and adaptability, much of your planning is wasted. All it takes is for one unforeseen event to occur and the plans are worthless. In addition, a plan without proper delegation, commitment, or follow-through is useless.

Often people jump right to "how" when considering some area of their life that they might want to change. We train our minds to problem-solve and so we jump right to "how." Clients will mention a dream they have about something, such as, "I want to fly a plane." And in the same breath talk themselves out of it because they have no idea how they would achieve it. Time and time again clients will jump from their dreams to not knowing how and they lose their excitement. They talk themselves out of the dream before the dream has a chance to germinate and take root!

Resist jumping to "how" as you self-discover. The strategy will come once you are clear about who you are and who you want to become. Figuring out "how" is easy once you know "who you are" and what you want.

First things first. You cannot devise a strategy for success until you know what success looks like. You cannot map out your route to success until you know your destination. And you cannot drive until you get behind the wheel.

Who

Conversations about who you are and who you are becoming require some skill, and often the people in your life don't know how to access the vocabulary for the necessary conversations to help you get to know who you really are, the person underneath all of the hats you wear. You are not your hats!

Over the years you focus your energy on developing what you've been taught is important. You build a career, buy a house, and have a family. And although these things are important and wonderful, they're not enough to fuel your soul. Your soul longs to be nurtured as well.

You long to connect with others and with yourself at a deeper level and yet you may not be sure how to do that or you fear being vulnerable so you settle for the superficial conversations. You get caught up in the story, in the drama of the moment. Or you hide in keeping yourself so busy you don't have time to think about who you are. Or you get caught up in what's going on for other people, not yourself.

What do I mean by going deeper? What do I mean by talking about the "who"? Let me give you an example. You see a friend you haven't seen in a while and she's lost quite a bit of weight. You compliment her on her appearance and then ask, "How did you do it?" But do you really need to know *how*? She tells you she's on Atkins, South Beach, Weight Watchers, or Jenny Craig. She tells you she's been going to the gym, working out with a personal trainer. Is this *really* what you want to know?

As smart and as educated as you are, you know what it takes to lose weight! Any method works if you put the time and energy into working the plan.

You could also ask her "why" she lost the weight but you already know the answer; she's committed to being a thinner person.

And although you might enjoy listening to her tell her story, what you're *really* thinking is, "What happened to make her *ready* to change her outward appearance? What made her willing to become someone different?"

Until you are ready, until you have a clear vision for something else in your life, until you eliminate the obstacles that hold you back from achieving that vision, until you fully commit to *being* someone different, it doesn't get done. And you spend time and energy beating yourself up for not doing it! And you get wrapped up in the story.

The question isn't *how* she did it, or *why* she did it, or *what* her story was to make her gain the weight in the first place; none of that really matters. The question is, *what inner shifts did she need to make in order to commit to becoming a thinner person?* And *who did she need to become* to allow the thin person within her to emerge?

After you envision what you want for yourself, your life, your career, your relationships, your kids, you need to ask the question, "Who do I need to become in order to achieve that vision or goal?"

If you want a great relationship, for example, what are the qualities of the person you'd like to meet or for your ideal spouse? Get really clear about the kind of person you want to spend time with. Make a list of thirty to fifty qualities that this ideal person would possess.

Next, consider the ideal relationship. What would the ideal relationship be like? What things would you be doing? How would you relate to one another? Describe this is an much detail as possible.

Finally, you need to ask yourself *who you need to be* in order to become the ideal partner for this relationship. This is the area you have control over. Become the person to whom your ideal mate will be attracted.

The "who" always has to do with the character and qualities of the person. It's their actions, roles, and stories that tell others about who they think they are and where they are on the continuum of their personal development.

When my son makes a mistake or chooses to lie about something, I ask him, "What does that say about the kind of person you are? Is that *who* you want to be?" It's not about the story of what he did, but rather who he is as a player in the story and whether that is who he wants to be.

My son learns that he has a choice about *who* he is and how he chooses to present himself to the world. He also learns that with each choice he makes, there are ramifications and consequences—sometimes good and sometimes bad. We learn from both. If he learns to consider the consequences of his actions beforehand, he can make his choices based on which consequences he wants to live with.

COACHING NOTE: Teaching Children to Make Good Choices

Teach your children how to make decisions for themselves rather than telling them what they should do. Help them learn how to process decisions by teaching them that every choice has a consequence. The consequences can be good or bad, what you want or what you don't want. You will need to reinforce this many times. If they make a choice, ask them what consequences they can expect to receive. Is that consequence something they want to have happen? Are they willing to live with those consequences?

Children, especially teenagers, need your help in learning how to think things through. They may want or need to hear how you would respond; they may not. It's not about you. Teenagers want and need to learn to think for themselves. If you give your child the tools they can use to make decisions, you help them accept responsibility for the actions they take and the choices they make.

Children need to define themselves as individuals. It's easy to tell a child what to do—what you think they should do. Take a minute instead to help them decide for themselves the kind of person they want to be, help them to identify and compare the choices available and choose based on which choice would be best for a person with those qualities. By doing this, you ensure your child grows to understand who he or she is, and learns to make decisions based on the identity they want to create for themselves. And as children learn to make good decisions for themselves, they grow to be adults who know how to make decisions that support them in creating a great life.

This doesn't just apply to children. You may find adults in your life who haven't learned how to make decisions for themselves. By helping others identify options and the consequences expected from those options, you assist them in learning how to make better choices for themselves without telling them what to do.

The "who" is the person behind the story. It's your identity. It's your true essence. The more aware you are of the qualities and characteristics you display, the more you can evolve yourself into the person you want to be. Your actions tell others and you a lot about who you are on your continuum of personal development.

In the next chapter, you will learn how to discover the person you are behind the story. Then you can learn what you need to do in order to evolve *who you are* so you can make decisions that honor the highest form of you. As you evolve, you tap into more of your potential—the person you are capable of becoming.

Coaching Challenge

- What area of your life is most frustrating to you right now?

- Is there a particular story of your life that you are attached to or that you identify with that keeps you living in the past?

- Is there any area in your life where you are struggling to figure out "why"?

- Practice being curious this week in your conversations with others. Use the questions introduced earlier in the chapter as a guide for participating in deeper conversations. Keep the conversation focused completely on the other person and see if you can help them to discover a piece of "who" they are.

Chapter Three

You Are a Puzzle

"The moment one gives close attention to anything, even a blade of grass, it becomes a mysterious, awesome, indescribably magnificent world in itself."
—Henry Miller, novelist

Have you ever put together a puzzle? First, you open the box and dump all of the pieces on a table. You spread them out. You pick up each piece one at a time, turn it over, observe it for shape, color, and a glimpse of something that might be useful, and then place it face up on the table.

As you turn over more and more pieces, a pattern emerges and the colors and shapes become familiar. You begin to see how some of them might fit together. And even before you've turned them all over, you might begin to put together those that fit. As more and more pieces are visible, you begin to get an idea of what the completed picture will look like.

Well, you are like a puzzle with each facet of you a piece. Think about it; your strengths, your values, your skills, and your talents each represent a piece of the puzzle. With each piece you discover about yourself, you get closer to uncovering the person you are. The clearer you are about who you are, the easier it is to make decisions about what you want in your life and the easier it is to design a life that brings you the most joy and fulfillment.

You want to know what your life purpose is. You want to know what you should do with your life and how you should live, hoping someone else has the answers to your riddle. We are taught at a young age to look outside ourselves for life's answers, and we're given plenty of rules to live by. But each of us must find our own path. Luckily, the answers aren't too far away. You just have to look within you. The more you know about *you* and act in accordance with your natural gifts, values, and strengths, the easier and more rewarding life is. Your purpose is revealed when you live in accordance with who you are.

Pieces of the Puzzle

To start uncovering the pieces of who you are, become an observer of yourself and simply pay attention to yourself in your daily routine. There is much you already know about yourself—what you like to do, what you're good at, your style, and your ability to communicate and navigate in the world. Start getting curious and create a list of one hundred things to know about you. Don't worry about how these things might fit together; like a puzzle, you may not see the pattern until you've turned over more pieces. For now, just explore.

Everything you do reveals something about who you are. The kind of work you do and the way you do it are pieces of your puzzle. Your work does not define you; it is an expression of who you are. The roles you play in life—your work, your position in your family, who you are as a parent, child, sibling, and spouse—and how you play those roles can be explored to provide you with pieces for your puzzle.

You are not your roles or your work; you are so much more. You are not your body; that is just your home. It's so easy to get caught up in these things. Go deeper by asking yourself some simple questions about *how* you perform these roles and what being in each of these roles means to you and your life. Observe yourself. What do your performance and your experiences tell you about who you are?

This is the self-discovery and acceptance process—understanding who you are, what is special about you, what is important to you, what you believe in. These are the first steps toward designing the life that brings you joy beyond your dreams.

Self-discovery is fun. There is no way around getting to know yourself; you must go through it. Attempting to avoid looking inward only leads to unhappiness and the feeling that there is something else—or something more—you are meant to do. This feeling comes when you know that you are not living up to your potential. It's an uneasiness that can translate into stress and inner turmoil, which can lead to physical disease and emotional distress.

Without Judgment

It's essential to look at each piece of you without judgment. Whatever it is, it just is. This is self-acceptance. Whether you like something or not, whether you think something is good or bad, is judgment. There is no place for judgment in self-discovery. Judgment can interfere with your ability to accept reality.

You might notice that as you identify something new about you, a voice inside you starts rationalizing it away: "I was taught not to boast, and anyway, everyone can do that." Your ego would have you believe that. The fact is you are who you are. If you are good at something, it just is. Don't judge it. Just recognize that there are things you are naturally good at. Don't assign meaning to it right now. If you come from a place of no judgment, then you are not explaining it or determining whether this piece of you is good or bad—it just is.

A Walk Through the Clouds: The Ego

Your ego is the story of you; it is your self-image, a picture of who you think you are. It's based on your conditioning and the meaning you've assigned to experiences in your life. The ego is a creation of the mind. It tells you who you should be. It thinks it's in control and wants you to think that too. It's *not* who you are. It's an illusion of you.

Your Inner Self is the true essence of *who you are*. Your Inner Self is life; it is love. This is separate and distinct from your ego. As you move through this book and start growing and evolving, you'll become stronger. The stronger your self becomes, the easier it will be to recognize the ego's imposition. The ego will fight to remain in control. It likes the status quo. Resist the initial temptation to give in to it. It's not real, even if it feels that way.

COACHING TIP: You are not your ego. You are a spiritual being having a human experience. Your Inner Self is your true essence. It is beautiful and loving. Your Inner Self requires care and nurturing. It wants to be fully expressed. By caring for yourself, living in integrity, and honoring the Inner Self—your true nature—you transcend the ego.

There will be things you discover that you are not good at; that's part of what I call "Club Human." You're not supposed to be good at everything; we're not designed that way. That is why we have each other. You need to identify your weaknesses so you can see how they impact your life, and then find ways to work around them, avoid them, or improve them if you must. Your weaknesses can also bring your attention to your greatest strengths. If you identify something you are *not* good at, what does that tell you about who you are, what you like, or what you *are* good at?

There need be no fear or struggle with this discovery. Address anything you might be resisting. Whatever you might resist now will persist until you are willing to face it and learn from it. Resistance usually means there's something you need to look at. Struggling is a choice. You can choose not to struggle. Just enjoy getting to know yourself at a deeper level. Imagine how much more you could accomplish in your life and how much more pleasure you will experience when you learn more about the capacity you have to live.

If there is any fear here, perhaps it's about how awesome life can be when you truly know yourself. Most people are brought up to believe that if things get too good something is bound to happen to mess things up.

But that's not true. It's all about what you believe. If you believe that life can be effortless and that you can learn to enjoy yourself, you will discover peace and happiness beyond your imagination. It is possible to give up a life of stress for a life of trust and faith.

You might find that you want to know *why* you are the way you are. A word of caution about asking the question "why": There may not be an answer, it may not be time for you to know the answer, or the analysis itself can distract you from discovering more about you. Focus on discovering what *is*.

Just enjoy getting to know yourself. Keep it light, playful, and fun. You are more than you think you are. And the more you know about your strengths, gifts, and talents, the more you can play with them!

When I was a recruiter, I interviewed hundreds of people. Many people had no idea what they wanted to do; they had an idea of things they might enjoy doing but never gave it the proper thought and consideration. Rather than looking inward at who they are and what they really wanted, they just applied for anything they thought they might be qualified for.

I worked for a long-term care (LTC) organization with several facilities in a metropolitan area and I remember speaking to one nurse who longed to work in pediatrics. What would she gain by working with the elderly in a LTC facility? How would that put her closer to her dream?

Another highly accomplished woman with numerous degrees came in to interview for a staff development position at one of the facilities. She had been recently laid off due to cutbacks. She said she wanted to teach. As I reviewed her resume, I saw that she had conducted research and many of her findings were published. She had advanced degrees and certifications. She had no experience in LTC. As we discussed this, it became clear that she undervalued her abilities and talents. She had no idea what she was worth or what she should be paid for her experience and knowledge. She was scared of being out of work. Her fears were driving her to seek the familiar security in a job—any job—rather than taking some time to look within to determine where she could best use her talents and skills.

The security she sought was to be found only within herself—her skills, education, talents, and abilities. There is no such thing as job security. You have to learn to be self-secure. In this example, this woman undervalued her accomplishments and experiential knowledge, as well as her education. By not recognizing her true worth, she was minimizing her strengths and her possibilities. She was living small. Your accomplishments tell a lot about who you are. You are *not* your accomplishments, however, and you are not your degrees or the long list of initials after your name. These things tell others something about what's important to you and your interests, the subjects you've studied, and the path you've chosen in your life, but they are "things"; they are not *you*.

Most people look for work in the same way. You look at the jobs available and decide whether that's the type of work you'd like to do. If instead, you first define who you are and what you want in a position, then you can look at the opportunities available for someone with your talents, strengths, interests, and skills. The opportunity you find *will fit you* rather than *you fitting into it*. Your work is an expression of who you are. If you don't know who you are or what you really want, then you will find yourself in positions that fall short of your desires.

If you are going through a career transition, visit our website at http://www.nurturingyoursuccess.com and under the Resources section, you'll find our "Job By Design" Worksheet to assist you in designing your ultimate job. It is structured to walk you through defining what you want before looking into the world for the answers.

See Yourself as You Are (aka The Reality Check)
"Be with what is so that
what is to be may become."
—Soren Kierkegaard, Danish theologian and philosopher

Keep your journal handy and write about the observations you discover about yourself as a way to get closer to the real you. Become the observer of your life and describe in your journal what you see. Do not judge; merely observe yourself throughout your day and discover who you are and *how you are being* in different situations. Self-discovery will lead you naturally toward change.

Once you start on your journey of self-discovery, you will find that it's an ongoing process. There will always be new things to learn about you. That is the beauty of life. Nothing stays the same for long. When you become naturally curious and wonder about your true self, you will see how incredible life is—how incredible you are—as is every other living thing on this earth. Learn to give your full self to the world. The world deserves to experience the best of you, just as you deserve all that life has to offer.

And when you think you've completed the puzzle, you'll find there is more to know about you. So you start anew. As time passes, you learn new things, you see things from a new perspective, and you add new skills. There's always some new piece of you to discover and some part of life to experience.

Getting curious about yourself is all there is in life. You cannot experience someone else's life. You are here to experience your own and to make some impact on this world. And you will make an impact. Your presence here leaves a mark; the world will be changed because you were here. You just need to decide how you want to make your mark.

Some people are afraid of self-discovery, scared at what they might find. There is nothing to fear. It is what it is. You are who you are. The very things you fear are the things you need to look at! Fear can hold you back from accomplishing more in your life—if you let it.

Fear is good. Like any emotion, it lets us know that there is so
thing that requires our attention. It is only as powerful as you allow it
to be. Learning all about you and how you work best—your mind, body,
spirit, emotions—that is what life is all about.

A Walk Through the Clouds: Denial

Denial is the inability or unwillingness to deal with or talk about
your feelings or the situation. It's when you look the other way. To deny
your feelings is to disempower yourself. You are giving your Inner Self
the message that your feelings are not important, that you don't matter.
By looking the other way, part of you believes it will go away on its
own. By refusing to confront the situation head-on, you actually permit the situation to have power over you.

Parents often do this with their children. They refuse to believe
that something might be amiss with their child. All the signs are there
and yet they deny themselves a look at reality. The child may be using
drugs; he or she may be suicidal or promiscuous. If parents would just
open their eyes, they could easily see the child's need for parental guidance, attention, love, and support. And yet the parents are too busy or
are denying the reality.

An analogy often used is the "elephant in the living room." In other
words, there is a monstrous thing right there in front of you, but you
deny it exists. You just keep walking around it, pretending it's not there.
If you open your eyes, you'll see the elephant—you can't miss it.

Ask yourself where you might be lying to yourself. Become willing
to be honest. After all, who are you lying to anyway? Who is it that is
affected by the elephant in the living room? You're the one sitting there.

Perhaps pride gets in the way. Perhaps it's fear. Whatever the cause
for the denial, it doesn't matter. Overcoming it and no longer permitting yourself to deny reality needs to be your focus now.

There's another form of denial, one that is a protective mechanism
of the mind that keeps us from seeing things we are not ready or willing
to accept, or deal with. This denial comes in the form of repressed memories from a terrifying event or trauma. This form of denial requires the
attention of a therapist who specializes in post-traumatic stress disor-
der. If there is something from your past that you feel is hidden from
you, get the professional support you need to overcome its grip. As long
as you continue to deny it, you remain imprisoned by it.

COACHING TIP: Becoming aware kills denial. Do not permit yourself to deny what is right in front of you. Do whatever it takes to handle the elephant in the living room in order to clear the way for better things. Whatever the cost of dealing with it cannot be worse than living a lie. It's like a thorn growing bigger and bigger until one day it stabs you so hard you can no longer deny it. Why choose to live behind a closed door refusing to look inside? Why wait until things get really bad before you must deal with them? How does that serve you? There's no good that comes of this. Choose to live with full knowledge and awareness of what is real. If you know there's something wrong with you medically, see a doctor. Whatever it is won't go away by ignoring it. If you know that you are unhappy in your marriage, deal with it head-on. You will find that in the end you are both happier because you faced it.

What are you denying in your life right now? Is there an elephant in your living room?

A Walk Through the Clouds: Avoidance

Avoidance is similar to denial. Whereas with denial, we deny the issue exists, with avoidance you know it exists but fail to deal with it.

The evidence is there. The debt is piling up but you fail to do anything about it. You're unhappy in your relationship, but if you admit it, you would have to do something about it. You hate your job, but it is easier to just go along with life as it is than to do what it takes to create a new reality.

Needing to be needed is an insidious form of avoidance. By focusing on what you can do for others and by busying yourself with caring for others, you avoid yourself. You hide in doing for others.

When you avoid something, you make a choice to do nothing about it. You see the elephant standing in the living room, but you continue, day after day, to walk around it rather than do the work to march the elephant out the door.

Brenda wanted to change careers. She made well over six figures annually, so the transition required careful planning to avoid a drastic dip in salary and lifestyle. Just when she was ready to switch to part-time in her current position to allow her more time to pursue her chosen field, she realized she couldn't make this change after all. She was very attached to the sense of security she had at her job because of how unhappy she was in her personal life at home. Her work, she discovered, was the only stable thing in her life; she'd been there more than a decade. She confessed at this time that the relationship with her husband was less than adequate; she and her children lived in fear—fear of his yelling, his anger, and his verbally and emotionally abusive behavior. A referral to the appropriate resource was made at this time.

Brenda knows something needs to be different and she is not ready to do anything to change it at this time. Until Brenda is ready to face the underlying issue and learns to feel comfortable and secure in *who she is* rather than looking for love and security *outside* her, until she is ready to move beyond the fear of possibly losing him and being alone, she cannot move forward with her dreams. As long as she avoids taking action in this matter, as long as she tolerates this behavior in her life, she chooses to dance around the elephant in the living room. Brenda has the power to remove this elephant—permanently. She needs to believe in herself, that she deserves to be treated with respect and love. Facing the truth and trusting that she has the strength and fortitude to move beyond this will free her and relieve the stress. The security she seeks is within; she needs to build up her inner strength, gather the support of a safe community of individuals, and garner her faith in a power greater than herself who will carry her through this time.

She needs to ask for what she wants. And she needs to no longer accept a life of fear. She needs to be willing to do the necessary inner work. Right now this situation is familiar; it's all she knows. There is another way to live. Brenda needs to love herself more than the illusion of love with this man. Fear is not love. People who love and respect themselves deeply do not yell and scream or force others to live in fear of them. She does him no favors by not teaching him this lesson. And the world loses out on receiving her talent because she is hiding behind this intense situation. Until she frees herself from this situation, she cannot move forward with her career pursuit. As long as she continues to accept this way of living, nothing will change. The moment she accepts that there is another way, that she deserves it, and she starts to take actions that support and honor her highest self, the universe will support her in going for what she wants. She, like each of us, is meant to find happiness and joy. There is no path to joy when living in fear.

Avoidance is a choice. Perhaps dealing with the issue is challenging. Perhaps you are concerned about the outcome if you face the elephant. Ask yourself, what kind of life are you living with an elephant in the living room? What are you really afraid of?

COACHING TIP: Taking responsibility kills avoidance. When you accept responsibility for all aspects of your life experience, you face everything. And what of the elephant? He gets walked out of the room to create space for new and wonderful things. This kind of change takes time so be patient with yourself. You didn't get where you are overnight. With each passing day you grow stronger and you move closer to living the life that brings you joy. You'll start to experience joy in the little things and in the peace that you've gifted yourself. We are here in this lifetime to experience the journey. The only destination in life is death, so don't be in such a rush. Enjoy each day and all its blessings. If you cannot find the blessings in today, what are you choosing not to see? Have you become comfortable with suffering?

Whatever you discover about yourself just is. When you deny that something exists or if you avoid dealing with something, you live under a lie that limits your capacity for happiness and fulfillment.

The Journey to Self-Wonder

> "I've gone through life believing in the strength and competence of others, never in my own. Now, dazzled, I discover that my capacities are real. It's like finding a fortune in the lining of an old coat."
> —Joan Mills, singer

There are really only two ways to get to know yourself better: Observe yourself and receive feedback from others.

In order to receive feedback from others, you need to ask. You cannot know the impact you make in the lives of others unless they tell you. And you might be very surprised. Ask others to share their thoughts, feelings, and ideas with you so you can learn what you mean in their lives, from their own perspective.

In discovering the pieces of your puzzle, you can observe your stories, you can observe your life situation, and you can observe your interactions with others.

Here are some ways to start you on your journey of self-wonder. Use your journal to write down your discoveries. Be patient with yourself. This kind of exploration takes time, but it offers a way of living in awareness every day for the rest of your life. There's no rush; go at your own pace.

- Pay attention to your feelings. Your feelings are your window to the world. They are your inner guidance system. What are they trying to communicate to you? Do not assign meaning to your feelings; just feel them.

- Become more aware of your thoughts and what you tell yourself. Your thoughts have created the person you are today. Control your thoughts and you change your life experience.

- Be aware of your behaviors. How do you respond in situations? Do you control your response or do you react without thinking? As you become more aware, you will learn to pause and respond with purpose.

- How well do you communicate with others? What is the language that you use? Do you talk just to talk? Or do you only speak with a clear purpose?

- Learning about yourself includes discovering how you impact others. How do others perceive you in social situations? What do others say about who you are to them? Look at your last several evaluations at work. What have your bosses and coworkers said about you? What are the compliments you have received over the years? These are hidden treasures that we often don't give enough attention. Compliments are how other people express what we mean to them. What a great gift to learn how we affect the life of another! Pay attention to what other people tell you about you.

COACHING NOTE: Receiving Compliments

How do you reply to a compliment? If you're like most people, you shrug it off by saying, "Oh, it was nothing." When you do this, you diminish your power. Learn to accept compliments gracefully by saying, "Thank you." And learn to use the compliment as an opportunity to self-discover. What is this person telling you about you? Often others have the keys to our talents. Something we do naturally well and without effort can be very challenging for others. This is where our gifts and talents exist. Ask them what was so pleasing to them about you and your work. Compliments are a wonderful gift.

- Do an attitude check. Are you positive and solution-focused? Or are you one of the complainers who always points out the negative in situations?
- What are your fears?
- What are those things/thoughts/actions that hold you back from achieving greater success in your life? Once you identify those things that stand in your way, you can learn to eliminate them.
- What makes you feel good? What are you passionate about? Become aware of the things you like and don't like.
- What is most important to you that without which your life would be empty? What do you value most?
- What are your strengths? What are those things that other people are always coming to you for? If you are not sure, ask others what they see as your strengths.
- Are there personal needs that are guiding your behavior? Do you need something from others such as the need to be right, the need for approval, or the need for recognition? Or perhaps like Brenda, are you looking for love and acceptance in all the wrong places? Identify them so you can accept responsibility for having those needs met once and for all.

A Walk Through the Clouds: Personal Needs

Personal needs are different from your physical needs for food, shelter, and clothing. We all have them at some time or another. Personal needs arise from some interpretation you made, usually in your childhood. Somehow you adopted the belief that you are not complete, that there is something missing that can only be filled by someone or something outside of you.

There are dozens of personal needs including the need to be right, to be cared for, to be loved, to be in control, to be needed, the need for acceptance, accomplishment, recognition, acknowledgment, appreciation, freedom, honesty, order, peace, power, safety, comfort, and clarity—to name a few.

When you have a particular need, it fuels your behavior. You'll do anything to get that need met, even choose unhealthy ways to get that need met. Needs must be satisfied.

The need to be right has fueled wars and fights. Give up your need to be right and you will experience less stress and more peace. Recognize that each person is right from his or her own perspective, and instead of making others wrong, focus on offering suggestions and new perspectives without attachment to the choices made by the other person.

Having a discussion with someone with a need to be right is fruitless and frustrating. You cannot rationalize or speak with someone's need. If you are willing to meet his or her need, you can say, "You're right," and then offer your perspective in the form of a suggestion such as, "Have you ever considered…?" Once the person's need is met, he or she will be open to hearing you. If you're not willing—and it's not your responsibility to do so—then the other person will be completely closed to hearing anything you have to say. You might as well end the discussion and have it at a later time when the need doesn't need to be satisfied.

The need for love and to please others has brought more lovers together in matrimony. This is where two people's "baggage" meets and there seems to be a fit so they get married. Marriages based on needs satisfaction are less than fulfilling and rarely last.

The pursuit of need satisfaction is one reason for many of our laws, which create boundaries and protection from the needs of others spilling into our space.

COACHING TIP: Personal needs can be eliminated. You can transcend your personal needs by understanding and accepting that you are whole and complete, that there is nothing missing from who you are. When you stop looking outside yourself for something or someone to complete you, you shift from neediness to needing less. You are able to trust in you and allow yourself to govern your behavior. When you are not being driven by unmet needs, you are able to live based in love for yourself and others, not driven by fear. When your personal needs no longer drive you, you're in a neutral place. Transcending needs does not create fulfillment. If you think of needs as a negative on a graph, then by transcending your needs you will be at zero. Not a bad place to be, but not fulfilling either. When you come from a place of completeness and wholeness, you are free to create a life where you express your values, strengths, gifts, and talents and live your passions. This fills you up.

The Picture in the Puzzle

There's a difference between who you think you are, who you are capable of becoming, and who others think you are. The process of becoming who you *really* are—your authentic self—will naturally close the gap.

As you look at the pieces of who you are and what makes you the incredible *you*, you'll start to see trends in your life and how things fit together. The more you observe about yourself, the more you see how *who you are* contributes to what you receive in your life.

What you *think* about you is different than who you are. This is known as your self-esteem. Let's put your self-esteem on hold for the time being. What I mean is, it doesn't matter what you think of you; your opinion doesn't matter. Remember, who you are is not what you do. If you are not happy with the things you do, then do something different.

When we consider who you are and we're describing the "who," there's no judgment. Your self-esteem is judgment. For now, suspend your judgment and stop thinking about how you feel or what you think about yourself.

You are a human being and that in itself is incredible. Add to that your unique qualities, your experiences, your blend of education, style, and background and you have the makings of a masterpiece. Who are you to judge that?

Just like the trees and the stars and the grass, you have a right to be here. And just like everything else in this world and beyond, you have a right to be all that is possible for you and to enjoy yourself.

Getting to know yourself better naturally translates into bigger and better goals and accomplishments. When you know who you are, you are more confident and make decisions that honor you. You accomplish your goals with amazing clarity, focus, and speed. You naturally move in the path of least resistance—the path toward authenticity, toward being the real you. When you commit to being your personal best, you design more effective plans, your desire drives your momentum, and you achieve the success you desire.

Explore without judgment—no good or bad, right or wrong—whatever you find, just is. And it's okay. As you come to know yourself better, you make better choices in your life, choices that bring you deeper levels of joy and fulfillment. When you are in alignment with who you are, you free yourself from trying to be someone you're not, or to fit into a mold someone else has designed for you. There is less stress. When you know who you are, your mind chatter quiets down. (Imagine that!) Your mind chatter is all of the stuff you aren't doing for yourself, ways that you are out of integrity, things you need to accomplish, things that you are putting up with, your needs, your values calling out to be noticed and acknowledged—all this stuff clogs up your brain so it keeps pouring out in the form of mind chatter. When you know who you are, you become more confident in being you. You fear less and you operate from a place of faith and trust. You believe in having fun and enjoying your life and you start purposefully making decisions that move you on the path to create a great life.

There are many things that get in the way of our creating a great life. We are taught to follow a pattern of rules set up by society. These rules exist to help and offer suggestions on how to live; however, they may not necessarily work for everyone. Learning to question the rules and to free yourself from the standards set by others is what the next chapter will teach you how to do.

Coaching Challenge

- Spend some time each day in self-reflection. In your journal, write down three new things you learn about yourself each day.

- Observe how you impact others in your life and work. Approach three people close to you and ask them to share with you what they like the most about you. What do they see as your strengths? What do you mean in their lives? You won't know unless you ask.

- Where are you hiding in denial or avoidance? What needs to happen for you to face everything?

- Are there any underlying personal needs driving your behavior?

- What are the gifts and talents you'd like to orient your life around?

Chapter Four

The Quest for Freedom

"The rules? They're more like guidelines really."
—Barbossa, *Pirates of the Caribbean*

When we speak with children, we ask them, "What do you want to do when you grow up?" Few people ask children "who" they want to be when they grow up. In fact, no one teaches children how to live in integrity or how to be their personal best. We don't teach children that what they do and how they do it is a reflection of *who they are*. Behavior is managed and children are taught *how* to do things. In fact, we learn how to "do" so much and so well that we become human "doings" and we don't really know how to be human "beings."

Our society encourages a life where you do more, faster, better. You are taught to give up your dreams to follow a path that will ensure you a better salary. Or your dreams are squashed by working so many hours that you have little energy for the other areas of life. Higher salaries and the accumulation of *things* are encouraged. You have credit cards for when you run out of your own money, and there are personal storage garages for rent when you accumulate more stuff than you can fit in your house. People don't learn to be financially literate, using bankruptcy as a way to escape responsibility for living a lifestyle beyond their means. And many people will never enjoy retirement because they neglect to plan properly.

Does this sound like happiness to you?

46

Then one day, after chasing a lifestyle for so many years, there's a longing that becomes evident. Somewhere inside you there's a feeling that you're missing something. Although most people like the status quo and will protect it at all costs, there comes a point when your heart overrides your head. "Settling" is no longer acceptable. You want more out of life.

In order to create an extraordinary life, you must learn to become a human *being* and connect with yourself at a deeper level. When you connect with your Inner Self, you unleash yourself from the facade, freeing yourself to become more. When you give yourself permission to go deeper, to be fully present, to live in integrity, to honor yourself, and to fully experience yourself and life, you become your authentic self.

Authentic people are attractive. We are naturally drawn to these people. Teenagers pick up on authenticity immediately. Teens will tell you whether someone is phony or not. And although teens may not have the language to express what authenticity means to them, they enjoy being around people who are their true selves. These people are good role models for teenagers.

Unfortunately, we are not taught how to be authentic as we grow up. We are taught to conform, to do as we are told. We do many things to ensure our children do as we want them to do, and be who we want them to be, rather than show them how to be their best self. In part, we don't live it ourselves; we can't teach what we don't know.

Years ago when I worked with teenagers in an acute psychiatric facility, I remember a wealthy woman complimenting her daughter on how beautiful she was because she was so thin. She made frequent comments to her daughter about her figure. Clearly, to this mother, being thin and beautiful was very important; she too, was thin and beautiful. She didn't realize, however, that by only focusing on being thin, she was projecting her own fears of being fat onto her daughter. Her daughter, unable to be her true self and feeling unloved for who she was inside, participated in self-deprecating behaviors including anorexia and heroin abuse. Her mother was actually setting her daughter up to hate herself. Her mother loved her for her appearance but shared little about the stuff that really matters. What this girl needed was to be loved unconditionally and she needed to be taught to love herself.

Societal Rules

> **"To be nobody-but-yourself—in a world which is doing its best, night and day, to make you somebody else—means to fight the hardest battle which any human being can fight; and never stop fighting."**
>
> —e. e. cummings, American poet and author

As a child, you are socialized by learning the rules of your family and society. You are taught what's acceptable, what's expected, and how to please your parents. You are taught how to be a good child, how to be successful at being a child. When you do something well, you are rewarded; when you do something wrong or bad, you may be punished or experience some other negative consequence for your behavior. It's important that children learn rules and limits to live by. After all, they don't know how to behave unless they are taught.

As you enter your teens, you challenge the rules. In your quest to understand who you are and what this "life" thing is all about, it's natural to begin to question the rules. You push the limits of your parents. You test the rules of society, too, in an effort to demonstrate independence, power, or control. You might drive fast, talk back to your parents, or stay out past your curfew. You might try to sneak into R-rated movies or do other things to prove you *can*. Often these are the years when teens try drugs, alcohol, or cigarettes as a form of rebellion. Many teens get piercings or tattoos as a form of self-expression and nonconformity with the rules.

Rock and roll was born from this rebellious state of mind. It was—and still is—a statement that rejects conformity and status quo for something dramatically different: The expression of self, of being different, or of celebrating the uniqueness of the individual. Rock and roll breaks the mold of civil obedience. With every generation there is a new kind of music that helps express the feelings of that generation.

What's fascinating is that every generation believes they are "different," that no one understands them when, in fact, every generation experiences the same feelings. This is the paradox of the generations: Although the world may look different today compared to what things were like when your parents were young, the struggles are the same. And just as you have a desire to break free from the rules, each person that came before experienced the same feeling of wanting to be different, wanting to do something unique, yet wanting to fit in. We are all very much the same. And this is the paradox of being human: You are unique and we are all the same.

As you move into your twenties, the rebellion subsides for more important issues, such as responsibility. Parents remind you that you need to find work to support yourself. Now that you are "grown up," you need to be on your own. There is this sense that you don't quite know what you're doing so you choose to follow the rules; after all, what do you know about being responsible at twenty years old? You conform, figuring that what works for others will work for you too.

But is it *really* working for others? You cannot look at someone's exterior and know what is going on inside.

We are taught how to be good children; how do we learn to be good adults? What does that mean anyway? What's the secret to living a successful life?

There is no secret; no one way works for everyone. Each of us must find our own truth. And each of us must find our own rules to follow. The rules are merely guidelines for you to follow until you are able to create rules that work for you. Learning to use your own level of integrity and your intuition—your own sense of knowing—are the true guides for living in alignment with your best self. Discovering and developing your integrity and intuition, trusting in yourself, and having faith in something greater than yourself is the grounding you need to move forward in life sure-footedly.

If, as a society, we knew better how to be successful at being adults, we would not have the divorce, suicide, and bankruptcy rates we have now. People would take more vacations, work less, play more, and experience less stress. Fewer people would rely on drugs or on medication to make them feel good or to deny their feelings. The fact is that we are more stressed out than ever and more people are in debt way over their heads than ever. Why does this matter? Because if we don't take care of ourselves, we become charity cases in our later years, or we must continue to work well into our retirement years because we lack the necessary funds to survive. If we don't learn to create rules that work for us, to honor ourselves and live in integrity, if we don't live our lives responsibly and yet in the way we want so we have fun and make the impact we want to make, we end up regretful. And we cannot get our time back.

Perhaps it's that we are just breaking the wrong rules. Scarring or abusing our bodies or getting ourselves in debt just because we can, produce the wrong outcomes. We are doing the wrong things for the right reasons but with disastrous results. Many of the rebellious behaviors of teens are dangerous and many people continue their self-destructive patterns well into adulthood.

Although some rules are designed to control your behavior or to make you behave in ways that please others or that are convenient for others, there are other rules that are meant to protect you from where other people, who have gone before, have discovered pain. These are the rules you adopt and follow because they allow you to honor yourself.

Instead of focusing on what rules to break, create a nurturing environment to learn to express yourself in ways that honor your highest self. Focusing on that will create the fulfillment you desire in a way that is healthy for you. When you choose to honor yourself, you take the focus off of the "rules" and place it on creating an environment that supports you in making good choices. It's not about conforming to societal rules, after all. It's about choosing the right rules for you to live by—the rules that help you create a great life!

Understanding the Rules

Rules are made up as we go along, designed because they make sense at the time. Aside from the Ten Commandments, nothing is written in stone. Given the level of awareness and the needs at the time, the rule makes sense. When we learn something as children, a way of acting or behaving perhaps, this makes sense to us because we don't know any different.

But rules don't always make sense and rules don't always fit for everyone. And over time, the rules may no longer apply.

Rules are static. They are inflexible. They tend to stay the same as changes go on around you. Something that was important for you as a child may no longer be good for you as an adult. And rules you adopt as an adult may no longer benefit you in the same way as you evolve and age. Rules can be limiting, forcing us to live beneath our capacities.

Rules can also provide a framework within which to live. This can be helpful and can provide some level of comfort. But rules that go un-challenged can be self-limiting.

As an adult, you accept full responsibility for you and for your life, for how you live, the choices you make, and the results you achieve. It's all about what you do with what you learned as a child. This implies that you need to evaluate the basic rules by which you live your life.

A Walk Through the Clouds: The Game of "Should"

"Life is too precious to get caught on a route that someone else chose for you without your even knowing it."
—Barbara Sher, American author

People often tell us how we *should* act, who we *should* be; everyone has his or her opinion (not that anyone asked for it). When you hear the word "should," take heed and consider what it is the person wants of you. Just because someone wants you to be a certain way, doesn't mean you have to become someone you are not. In what ways are you living up to the *shoulds* of others?

"Should," "supposed to," "have to," and "ought to" are red flags that signal you are about to be told to do or be a certain way. As a responsible person, you have the power to question and to decide whether this is you or not. Not only do you have the power but you have a responsibility to yourself to question who you are and how you want to be. After all, this is your life you are living, isn't it?

In what ways are you *should*-ing others? Perhaps you are telling other people who they *should* be. A man attending a recent presentation asked, "What if I really don't like how my coworker changed her hair, are you saying I shouldn't tell her that she should wear it the other way?" It really depends on the intention and the way you phrase your com-ments. If your intention is to let her know she is beautiful and that you prefer the other way, that could be acceptable. If your intention is that she should change her hair to suit your pleasure, that's different. The bottom line is that it doesn't matter what you think, it only matters what makes her happy.

Whenever you are about to *should* someone, phrase it in the form of a suggestion: "Perhaps you'd like to…" or if it's a strong request, "You need to...." By pausing first to consider your intention for what you're about to say, you learn to become a more effective communicator.

In what ways are you *should*-ing yourself? When you *should* yourself, you place unrealistic demands on you. Focus instead on honoring yourself. Instead of acting in ways that you think will make others happy, reach into your own heart and start making choices that bring you happiness and make your heart dance. Stop *should*-ing yourself and you are free to become who you want to be.

This is one way to question and challenge the rules.

COACHING TIP: Life is short. A life spent listening to the whims of others will not bring you the happiness and fulfillment you seek. Take notice of how other people tell you who you should be and choose to do what makes you happy. Stop letting people should you!

Kira wanted to lose weight. "I know I could lose weight if I would eat home-cooked meals, but I don't like to cook." Kira grew up under the belief that women were supposed to cook. She hated to cook so she avoided the kitchen completely and eating became a chore, something she did on the way to something else. This meant she mostly ate fast foods, which is how she claims to have gained weight.

"What if you decided that it is okay for you to *not* cook," I challenged. "How would life be different if you accepted the fact that you don't like to cook with no judgment?"

There was silence on the other end of the phone.

If Kira could let go of this rule, she could create a new rule based on what is true for her. If she knows she doesn't like to cook and she accepts this without judgment, then she can give herself permission to do what feels good, in this case, to *not* cook. Then she can make decisions around food that honor her. This is one example of *The Journey Called YOU*— becoming more aware of some aspect of you, accepting it for what it is, making choices that honor you, and giving yourself permission to write new rules that make you happy.

Once Kira let go of the unwritten rule that governed her life, she could then create a life around food that worked for her. She gave herself permission to *not* cook and then we discussed alternatives to fast food. She needed to define what role food would play in her life and how she wanted to experience food every day. Instead of running away from food and gobbling it down to eliminate the hunger pains, she decided to make food an enjoyable part of every day, focusing on providing her body with the nutrition it needs in a way that honors her. Kira will lose weight as a byproduct of focusing on "who" she is, her relationship with food, and making healthy choices that honor her body.

Checking in on Habits

"I am your constant companion.
I am your greatest helper or your heaviest burden.
I will push you onward or drag you down to failure.
I am completely at your command.
Half the things you do, you might just as well turn over
     to me,
And I will be able to do them quickly and correctly.
I am easily managed; you must merely be firm with me.
Show me exactly how you want something done, and after
a few lessons I will do it automatically.
I am the servant of all great men.
And, alas, of all failures as well.
Those who are great, I have made great.
Those who are failures, I have made failures.
I am not a machine, though I work with all the precision
     of a machine.
Plus, the intelligence of a man. You may run me for profit,
or run me for ruin;
It makes no difference to me.
Take me, train me, be firm with me
And I will put the world at your feet.
Be easy with me, and I will destroy you.
Who am I? I am HABIT!"
—Ed Hirsch, business expert

Humans are creatures of habit. The conscious mind can only hold one focus in the moment. It's therefore very efficient for us to create routines. In this way, we don't need to pay attention to a process that becomes so familiar. By not having to focus on each step every time we do something, our minds can focus attention on other things. This makes us more efficient by freeing up time and energy—our personal RAM—for something else.

Once we learn to do something a certain way, the habit sticks with us and can continue on for years without being checked. Even our cars require regular servicing, as do our bodies through doctor visits and exercise. Our habits need to be checked as well. After a while, they may not be as efficient as they could be. Becoming aware of our habits permits us to challenge them.

Habits can be things you think, do, or say (to others and yourself). Identify your habits by simply noticing things about yourself. Become aware of little things you do during the course of a day. It may be easier to ask whether the results you are achieving are bringing you the success you want and then looking at the process you use to bring about that result. Yes, it will take some effort on your part to become aware of everything you think, do, and say. Every time you brush your teeth, eat a meal, or take a shower you do it the same way. The route you travel to work is the same and you know the route home so well that you make the drive without thinking about it. Have you ever arrived home and wondered how you had gotten there? It was as if your body went through the motions without your needing to think about what to do. (This means, of course, your attention was elsewhere. Scary thought, huh?)

Unless you create a consciousness around it and learn to do something differently, you will respond to situations, manage your time, and react emotionally to things in the same way every time.

Start experimenting with change. Shake things up a bit and start doing things differently. Take a moment to consider your response before you proceed as usual. Don't just do things because you've always done it that way. Ask yourself why you do it the way you do, what results it brings you, whether those are the results you want, and whether there might be a better way.

EXERCISE: The Shower

The next time you take a shower, do it backward. Taking a shower is something you do so often that you will do it subconsciously, without thinking about it. Shake things up a bit by bringing your actions into consciousness. If you normally start by washing your hair, wash your elbows instead. Then your feet and then your hair, back, legs, and face. Take the shower differently than you normally would and you will see how uncomfortable it is. But it's just different, not painful.

If you decided that you wanted to change the way you showered permanently, it would be challenging because each time you got in the shower you would need to force yourself to pay attention to what you are doing, otherwise you would naturally go back to your default method of shower-taking. You would need to keep the new actions conscious until you created a habit of this new way of showering. Yes, changing a habit takes some time and effort, but it's not impossible.

By trying an exercise such as this, you will see how it feels to pay attention to your habits, the things you do automatically. You'll find it somewhat awkward but with the right attitude, you can have a lot of fun.

The Young Adult Shift

At some point in your young adulthood, in your twenties or early thirties, a shift takes place (hopefully) whereby you mentally become an adult. It's that moment when the realization hits you and you "get" it.

For me, it happened when I was twenty-five. I was speaking with a physician on the psychiatric unit where I worked and it occurred to me that he was listening to what I had to say. He was interested in my opinion. I realized at that moment that I was, in fact, an adult and the difference between us was education and age. What this meant for me was that I could do anything, be all I was capable of being. And the first question that popped into my head was, "If he is a physician and he's listening to me, how much more do I have to offer? What can I do to be more of who I am capable of becoming?"

The other shift that occurs in your young adulthood is the shift from seeking approval from others to seeking approval from yourself. Usually, this moves you from seeking parental approval to seeking your own approval. Again, this is a step into self-responsibility. It's accepting responsibility for your own life and what you do with it.

I remember this moment in my life very clearly. I had a choice to make and my father made it very clear what he expected me to do. It was a decision, however, that I could not make and we disagreed. He was thinking practically. And although I am a practical person, I was coming from a different perspective and viewed the situation differently. Clearly, this was a test of my own personal integrity. I could not choose his recommended course of action, which put my father and me at odds. But as fate would have it, the issue went away and it became a nonissue. However, I knew something had changed within me. I felt different, more confident, and self-assured. I was whole and I was able to accept full responsibility for my actions then and in the future, regardless of what it meant other people thought of me. I decided that I could not live my life based on what pleased others. At the end of the day, I was the one who had to live with my decisions; I had to please myself.

A Walk Through the Clouds: People Pleasing

Many people focus their energies on pleasing others. By pleasing others, you feel good about yourself. By pleasing others, you also follow the unwritten rule that you should care for others first and then yourself.

This unwritten rule can be found governing the actions of many parents, caregivers, and those in the helping professions. Somehow the belief is adopted that doing for others is nobler than caring for oneself.

The problem with this comes when you people-please to the point of your own detriment. You become resentful and angry. You have little time for yourself, to do the things you want to do. Life is happening all around you and you're too busy making things right for others that you fail to realize how your life—your time—is slipping away.

By not taking care of yourself first, by putting others before yourself, you tell yourself that you don't matter, that what you want is unimportant. You create limits to your happiness and you create your own ceiling for success.

It also means that you may not be taking the best care of yourself. Only by taking care of yourself can you be in the best condition to care for others. You need to please yourself first.

Also, when you focus always on other people, they can learn to take advantage of you. If you are always there to do for them, then there is no impetus for them to do for themselves. This causes dependency and it doesn't promote other people's accepting responsibility for themselves.

COACHING NOTE: Being Responsible for Children's Actions

When your children are young, you are responsible for their behavior. During the teenage years, however, children need to learn to become responsible for themselves so they can accept full responsibility for themselves as adults. If you continue to enable your children by supporting them and cleaning up their messes after they are well into adulthood, you create dependency, setting your children up to need you to do for them rather than helping them accept responsibility and take the driver's seat in their own life.

COACHING TIP: It's wonderful to please others. As a parent myself, I know what it means to put kids first, but not at my own expense, not to the point where I only care about him and not about myself. You have the right to please yourself, do what you want and what makes you feel good, and learn to say no when it no longer feels good. In fact, use your own feelings as a guide to determining how much to do for others. No matter how much you do for others, if you are not doing what you need to do for yourself, you will have to endure the consequences of your actions—or lack of action. As long as you are pleased with how you are spending your time and with the results you are achieving, then wonderful. But refrain from using other people's reactions to govern your behavior and your choices.

Marsha was fifty-eight and looking for new employment after a downsizing left her unemployed. As a nurse, she had spent her life caring for others. Now she was having difficulty making ends meet during this transition because she had no financial reserves set aside for herself. She had always given so much to others, particularly her children. Marsha never planned ahead for what she might need to care for herself and she never learned to pay herself first. Without planning in life, things rarely get accomplished. Now, she is financially strapped (a scary place at any age), and she will need to work well beyond retirement age for she has no funds to support her.

When we avoid taking care of ourselves, we are not being responsible.

Without accepting full responsibility, we tend to place blame and look for others to hold responsible for our mistakes or choices. This is not effective. It places others in charge of your life. It means that you lack the control or power to affect your world and we know that's not true. In fact, you alone have the power to change your life, whether it's your relationship with your kids or spouse, your level of stress, or the amount of money you have; you have the power to create your life—and to recreate it.

Many people fail to make the shift to seeking approval from themselves and continue to seek approval from some external source—in peers, in bosses, in a spouse, or still from their parents. You cannot find the key to your happiness or success in the eyes and mind of another. I'm not suggesting that you stop wanting others to like you or the choices you make. What I am saying is that you have to do what's best for you. You have to make choices based on what you want your life to be about and not make choices solely to please others. If you do, happiness will always be elusive.

The Unwritten Rules

When you are young and "being socialized," you learn to meet other people's expectations. You establish beliefs based on your environment, cultural norms, and the interaction of the individuals in your home and community. You learn that this is the way it's done—the customs that are followed, the way people talk to one another, the way men treat women and women treat men, and the way men and women treat themselves. You learn how to be, what's appropriate, and what outcomes occur as a result of those behaviors.

Sometimes you learn how you don't want to be based on the behaviors of others. I remember when I was growing up my father's desk was always so full of paper. It wasn't messy; there were just piles and piles of paper. All that paper scared me! As an adult, I don't make piles and I am quick to file loose papers. I also don't store a lot of papers. I tend to dump them rather than keep them. Whereas my dad has paperwork going back three decades (or more!), I save only a few months or years of important documents.

This is just one small example of who I am, based on what I witnessed as a child. I know this about myself because it was easy to relate this back to how I grew up. Often, we don't know why—or perhaps, we don't really want to know why we are the way we are. And as we dis-cussed earlier, it doesn't really matter "why" you do things as you do; it matters what you decide is best for you and that you live in accordance with the choices that best suit you.

We spend our lives trying to understand who we are based on how we grew up! It's amazing how much of an impact the formative years play on who we become and how we think and relate in the world.

When you're growing up, you learn to measure up to other people's standards and expectations of the rules that are important to them. It's important that you are taught rules and standards by which to live. You also interpret things you observe or hear in such a way that creates beliefs under which you learn to live. The intention may not have been to limit you. Also, people don't always know the impact of their ac-tions or comments. Something said in jest or in earshot of a youngster may not have been intended but still impacted you. Words are never innocent; there's always an impact.

As an adult, you either continue to live by the standards, rules, and beliefs you learned as a child, change them to suit you, or create your own standards. You may live in fear of changing the rules or of even questioning the rules, worried about fear of rejection, fear of conse-quences (real or imagined), or fear not being liked. You learn to please others and to focus your life on doing what you are told and on what's expected. Unless you start setting your own standards and expecta-tions for yourself, you will continue to live under the ceiling created by trying to live your life's questions using someone else's answers.

A Walk Through the Clouds: Limiting Beliefs

Limiting beliefs are statements or beliefs that convince you that you can't be, have, or do what you want. They are anything that limits your ability to have your dreams come true.

Often these limits are set when someone tells you something, per-haps when you were a child, and you interpret it to mean that you cannot have more or be more. It may be that they themselves use these limiting statements in their own life and we unwittingly perpetuate their use. "You can't do that. That's too hard. You're not good enough or smart enough."

When we are young we are impressionable. We listen to our elders, especially our parents, and when something is said—even in jest—we easily use that information to create boundaries for ourselves. These boundaries are what we use to guide our behavior. Often, we set these boundaries too low and we don't reevaluate these beliefs as we become adults.

Even as adults we can be unwittingly limited by someone's remarks. People who are jealous or envious or simply tactless may make a comment that we take to heart. After I had been diagnosed as hypothyroid (causing a slowing of the metabolism leading to slowing of the bodily functions, fatigue, weight gain, hair loss, and so on), I had been steadily gaining weight. I was worried since nothing I did seemed to matter, and I spoke to my physician about my concerns. He responded by telling me that I would never be able to lose weight and not to worry about it. I found that remark insensitive and decided to change physicians but I internalized those comments and realized years later that they had become limiting beliefs for me. Once I started to believe that I could lose weight and began visualizing the weight leaving my body, I was able to lose some of the weight I had gained during those years.

You may have been taught that you will never get ahead no matter how hard you work. You are supposed to be modest or to not think too big. Perhaps you are expected not to surpass your parents, siblings, or spouse in amassing wealth or having a better career. Women were often brought up under a ceiling that men are superior and they need to put their husband's needs ahead of their own. These beliefs keep you operating under a ceiling.

We are also limited by our expectations of the way life should be, by our education, our experience, our culture, our religion, and so on. Many who have dared to dream something beyond the norm were shunned for their belief in the impossible, but their persistence and determination made the improbable possible, like Thomas Edison and the light bulb. And yet, it is in the possibilities, the ideas that reach beyond what we expect or know to be true, that we uncover new realities, discoveries, and inventions.

COACHING TIP: Change the things you tell yourself about what you are capable of achieving. Become aware of your limiting beliefs and then use your internal dialogue (the way you talk to yourself) to train yourself to move beyond these self-imposed limitations. Then you can shift to beliefs that expand the possibilities. What if there were no limitations?

Remain open to the possibilities. Be curious about the potential that things could be different from what you think. Investigate. Do not rush to say, "That can't work." Ask instead, "How can that become possible?" Recognize that limiting beliefs can be challenged and changed. You can decide to think something different. And in thinking differently, you can change the world. "I can't afford that!" becomes "How can I afford that?" And, "I'd love to have that job." becomes, "Who do I need to become in order to land that job?" Empower yourself by how you speak to yourself, by your attitude, and with your vision for success.

If you hear yourself or others say, "Well, that's just the way it is." Or, "It has to be done this way." Start challenging it. The first step is to become more aware. Then you can start to identify other ways of doing or being and decide which way works best for you. In this way, you give yourself the power to choose. Without awareness, you don't have a choice; you just act in response to a familiar set of triggers, like a Pavlovian dog or a robot on autopilot.

Learn to become more aware of the rules that govern your behaviors. This will bring to your consciousness the beliefs that rule your life. You have every right to question them, challenge them, and decide for yourself what rules or assumptions you want to follow, which rules you want to change, and which rules you want to throw out completely.

What if you could really do what you've been dreaming about? That's exactly what happened with Mindy's husband, Fred. Fred had been very involved in sports in his youth. He'd coached ball for many years but had been working in a corporation for the past nine years until recently when he was laid off. Mindy called to ask, "Could he go back to coaching sports after all those years? Is he too old? Has he been out of the game for too long and should he look for another corporate job?"

My response: "He needs to do what brings him the most joy and what allows him to maximize his strengths and express the passion inside of him." Honestly, he wouldn't know if he was able to return without getting out there and asking!

Fred did receive an offer for a high school coaching job, which he gladly accepted. He is now doing what he loves, the family has recently moved, and they are very happy. When one partner in a relationship gives the other permission to pursue his or her dream, they both win.

Challenging the Rules

"If we do not rise to the challenge of our unique capacity to shape our lives, to seek the kinds of growth that we find individually fulfilling, then we can have no security: we will live in a world of sham, in which our selves are determined by the will of others, in which we will be constantly buffeted and increasingly isolated by the changes round us."
—Nena O'Neil, American anthropologist and author

People throughout the centuries have challenged rules and beliefs; some were even killed for it. But in the questioning, they uncovered new worlds of discovery and thought. The world was thought to be flat until the notion was questioned. In the early 1900s, Ignaz Semmelweis suggested that doctors and midwives wash their hands at childbirth. This was before germ theory was discovered. He didn't know "why" it worked but it did and it was years before it was proven scientifically. This simple change in practice saved lives.

The United States was founded by questioning and challenging the rules of England. The U.S. Constitution declares that people have the right to life, liberty, and the pursuit of happiness. The end of Apartheid and the tearing down of the Berlin Wall are other examples of throwing out the "story" of the way it has always been in favor of something new and the possibility for a different future.

Challenging the rules and assumptions by which you live can be a lot of fun. What it means is asking yourself whether what you are doing makes the most sense for you. People are often under the impression that you shouldn't question anything. It's never bad or wrong to question a rule, even if others would have you think that. Rules have a way of closing us in, forcing us to succumb to ways of living that do not necessarily suit our needs. The rules are merely guidelines for you to adapt to what works best for you. As long as you remain in integrity and honor yourself, you won't be disrespectful to others. You may make choices that others don't agree with; you cannot live your life based on another's ideas for how your life should be.

If you could throw out all of the rules and start over, which rules would be the first to go? What would you choose instead?

Mary had been married for many years before she got up the courage to leave her husband. She had considered leaving many times over the years. Her religious beliefs had held her back from leaving sooner as well as concerns over what others would think of her if she were divorced. The marriage was anything but fulfilling. Her husband was very suspicious and demanding. She lived in a small prison, experiencing very little freedom to be herself or to do the things she enjoyed.

When she questioned her religious beliefs, she realized that her higher power, whom she called God, wanted her to be happy. She questioned her beliefs about divorce and her understanding of what marriage should be versus what she wanted it to be versus what her marriage was like (her reality). She decided that what mattered to her was that she learns to fully express herself, which she identified was not possible in this marriage. When she realized this, it was easy for her to see that her religious beliefs could be challenged and that she could make decisions based on what was best for her. In doing so, she honored God. In fact, by not living her best life, she was actually shunning God. This did not make her less religious; it actually forced her to look at how she viewed God, how she practiced her religion, and how she interpreted her religious views. Sometimes it's not the rules that are confining but rather people's interpretation of the rules. And that can be your interpretation or someone else's they are imposing on you. Any individual, organized body, government, or institution that imposes rules that are unbreakable, especially when those rules are not in the best interest of the individual, is taking away your right to personal freedom and free will, the one gift that is bestowed upon us all. (An individual who imposes unbreakable rules on another that do not serve their best interest could be considered abusive.)

Mary learned that by questioning and challenging the rules, lightning did not strike her down. Nothing bad happened. In fact, she feels more in charge of her life. She is free.

A Walk Through the Clouds: Fears

"We all experience doubts and fears as we approach new challenges. The fear diminishes with the confidence that comes from experience and faith. Sometimes you just have to go for it and see what happens. Jumping into the battle does not guarantee victory, but being afraid to try guarantees defeat."
—Brian Goodell, Olympic gold medalist

Fear shows up in many different ways. It learns to disguise itself under the guise of rules and "shoulds." There is the fear of success, the fear of failure, the fear of power, or the fear of responsibility; there is fear that the outcome will be worse off than the way it is. I find that most people are fearful of being great, of what others will think if they become more self-expressed, or of what that will mean to their relationships. If you allow yourself to be great, then how will others handle it?

There are really two types of fear. One is the fear that sends us into the body's natural fight or flight response. This fear occurs in response to the threat of danger. It needs to be acknowledged and requires your attention.

The other fear, the kind of fear that if you flipped it over would blaze of excitement, is the one you want to look at more closely. This fear is not real. This is the fear experienced when your toe is touching the edge of your comfort zone. This is good fear. It's just a little self-doubt. It signals that you are stretching yourself, forcing yourself to extend beyond the safe boundaries of the known and accomplished and into the unknown and the possibilities.

Embrace your fear. Feel it. Experience it fully. Learn to respect its purpose. And then let it go. Muster your courage and move forward in spite of your fear. Move forward in faith.

COACHING TIP: Acknowledge your fear and allow yourself to experience the heart of it. As you do, you will notice the feeling drift away and excitement take its place. When you notice and acknowledge your fear, you respect it. When you run from your fear, you make it bigger and it continues to grow until you acknowledge it or eliminate the trigger, which is the movement to the edge of your comfort zone. If you stay in your comfort zone and never allow yourself to cross into the unknown, you'll live a safe life. But it will be very shallow. If you need support, then find a therapist or coach to take this walk with you. You don't need to travel alone.

What are some of the rules you grew up with that are still governing you? List some of the messages you grew up with in your journal.

- Do as I tell you.
- Don't ask questions.
- If you make a mistake, you'll go to hell or be struck by lightning.
- If you love me then you'll do....
- Your father is always right.
- Your mother is always right.
- Listen to authority figures—don't challenge them.
- What do you know? You're only a child. You don't know anything.
- Your feelings don't matter. Use your head.
- Don't cry.
- Keep your mouth shut.
- Don't be different.
- Don't rock the boat.
- Children are to be seen, not heard.

Some people grew up under rules that were cruel and thoughtless. Horrifying as they may sound, people do say them. As you read through the ones listed below, resist the temptation for asking why or for placing judgment. Just bring them into your awareness and identify the ones that you can relate to. Then you can choose to create new beliefs to guide your life.

Do you identify with any of these? Write your own in your journal.

- You're stupid. You're ugly. You're fat....
- You can't do anything right.
- You should be ashamed of yourself
- I hate you.
- You're nothing.
- You'll never turn out to be anything.

What about things that you learned, not by what was said, but by the way things were done. In your journal, list some of the things you witnessed as a child growing up.

- Not following up or finishing things once started.
- Breaking promises.
- Not using manners with family members.
- Yelling or cursing in the home.
- Hitting, throwing things, or other disrespectful behaviors.
- Lack of praise.

Although many people today live in single-parent homes, there is still much to be learned from the interaction between a man and woman. What are some of the spousal, relationship, or male/female interactions that you witnessed? In your journal, list some of the messages that you learned about men and women in relationships.

- Women do the cooking, cleaning, take care of the kids, run the home, and work full-time. Men just work full-time.
- Women don't talk back to men.
- Women say yes...regardless.
- Women must please men.
- Men must bring home the money (i.e., women cannot make more money than men).

Children need structure, rules, and expectations. They need rules from which to learn boundaries and right from wrong. As adults, we must question the rules that we came to understand as children so we can determine whether they are relevant for us as adults. What are the rules that govern your actions? Do these rules work for you? Do they allow you to live your best life? Or do they limit you in ways that do not honor your ability to enjoy life, liberty, and the pursuit of happiness?

Often the rules or messages you learned in your youth go unchallenged until you have children of your own and you start imposing rules on them. You question what you are teaching them and what you really want them to learn.

You don't need to wait to have your own children or for some other external event, such as the death of a parent, to create an impetus for examining the rules in your life. Use your power to become aware and pay attention to how you do the things you do and whether the results you are experiencing bring you joy and happiness.

The fact is that when people break the rules, we admire them. We admire their ability to be themselves and break away from the ritualistic mentality. People who express themselves and their own style in their own way possess this air of confidence that tells the world how comfortable they are with themselves. There's not arrogance or defiance about breaking the rules, but rather a commitment to being yourself and doing what's best for you.

Your job as an adult and as an employee is to challenge the status quo. It's the only way new things are created and new worlds are discovered.

When you start questioning the rules by which you have learned to live, you start to identify those things that no longer serve you. Once identified, you can eliminate those beliefs, thoughts, traditions, and behaviors. This creates space, an openness and freedom for you to think differently, behave differently, and create new outcomes for your life.

In the next chapter, we continue our journey by questioning your beliefs about success. What does success look like for you? Without a vision for success, how will you know what you are working toward? How will you know when you've achieved it?

Coaching Challenge

- Is there any area in your life where you are rebelling against some unwritten rule? What if you were to stop rebelling and start creating new rules to guide your behavior? What rules could you adopt that would support you in being who you want to be?

- Are you still seeking approval from another for your choices in life? What would it be like if you looked inward for your own approval?

- What are the limiting beliefs that are creating ceilings for your success? What beliefs could you adopt instead that would expand the possibilities for you?

- Are there any fears that hold you captive? Are you living under the fear that if you challenge the rules something bad might happen?

Chapter Five

A Vision for Success

"You were designed for success. You were endowed with the seeds of greatness. But would you know success if it tapped you on the shoulder and gave you its business card?"

—Zig Ziglar, author and motivational speaker

Consider your beliefs about success. What does it mean to be successful? Who do you know who has achieved high levels of success? What is it about that person and his or her life that you admire?

Success is an outcome. You cannot "be" success. You "have" or "achieve" success. To succeed is to realize a favorable result, the attainment of a desired goal. But there are many people who achieve what they thought they wanted only to find themselves just as empty as before they started.

What is success?

Perhaps it can be found in your *being* a certain way. If you look at the kind of person you are "being," rather than what you have or don't have, you can determine whether you are living a quality life or not. Perhaps what we are searching for isn't success at all but something else entirely.

Perhaps what we seek is the feeling of contentment with life, peace of mind, and happiness, that feeling we feel when we know we are living exactly the life we are meant to live, no longer struggling against what is. Perhaps it's that feeling you feel when you know that you are transparent, that you are completely okay with who you are right now even as you continue to evolve. What each of us chooses to do in order to achieve this state would certainly make one successful. What we are really saying when we speak of success is, *what will success feel like and what will you be doing when you achieve that state of being?*

Why is it important to define success for yourself? For each of us, success looks and feels different. When you don't know what you are after, you often get things you don't want or you want things you don't need. And when you have no destination in mind, any road will get you there.

Advertisers spend a lot of time, energy, and money creating needs. That's what keeps them in business; they create perceived needs to get you to purchase products. "Come in now to purchase the newer, better, faster model!" It's easy to become seduced by the thousands of advertisements that hit you throughout the course of a day. But we all know that getting more doesn't make your life easier. The paradox of the 21st century is that with all of the technology we have today, our lives are more complicated than ever. And we are more stressed out because of it.

There are many people in your life who have their own agenda as to who you should be and what a successful life should be for you—your boss, coworkers, friends, spouse, parents, and siblings. It's easy to become distracted by the needs, desires, and fears of others when you don't have an agenda of your own.

Something happens—a death, a layoff, or a job termination. Perhaps it's the midlife thing or a life-threatening illness that arouses you to stand up and take notice. Perhaps nothing triggers it; perhaps you just wake up one day, look around, and ask yourself, "How did I get here?" And perhaps more importantly, "What am I doing here? Should I be doing something else with my life?"

By questioning your vision of success, you determine what success will look like for you. When you know what success means for you, then it's easier to determine how to go about achieving it, and you'll be better able to gauge whether you are living the kind of life you want to be living.

If we learn from the dying, what they share about life is that they wish they had taken more risks in doing the things that they wanted to do—taking that vacation or buying that rental property. Never do they share that they wish they had worked more or had more money or a bigger car. They wish they had taken better care of their bodies. They wish they had done more with their time—seen more. They are grateful for the love they shared and the relationships they had with family and friends. Some wish they had spent more time with those they loved and let go of grudges sooner. They tell us not to wait to do the things we enjoy; time has a nasty habit of passing all too quickly. And they all speak of how they hope their lives mattered in some way, that their existence on this planet has left it a better place for them having lived.

I remember many years ago reading a short story called "Harry Would Have Loved This." It was about a woman on a trip to Hawaii. In the story, she describes all of the wonderful things she sees, tastes, and experiences, and how Harry would have loved it. Harry was her husband and often spoke of his dream to go to Hawaii. But he never made the time; he was always too busy. After he died, she went on the vacation alone.

People who dread the passing of the years often feel as though they are not truly living. They fear getting older because they know that their time is limited. As death nears, they begin to feel their mortality and bargain for more time so they might do something meaningful. If they only had more time, then they would do something great.

They've not yet learned that the beauty of life is in being present for what is. The beauty of life is in the little things, the everyday things. It is in the smell of a flower, the laughter of a child, the smile of a friend. The destination will always be death; no one escapes this existence alive. We are temporary and everything in this life is temporary. It's the journey we travel, the choices we make, and how we enjoy our time that make life worthwhile.

What will a successful life be like for you? When you lie on your deathbed, what do you want to be able to say about the life you've had? You can be proactive and design your life experience, living each day to its fullest, or you can cross your fingers and hope for the best. The choice is yours.

Whatever you choose, you cannot go back and correct what you've done. You can only look to today and what you can do to make today great and to bring about a better, more fulfilling tomorrow.

Many people focus on what they have or how bad it is, how they wish it were different. This will only keep things the way they are.

Success begins with a vision or a dream for what is possible for you. Greatness is created and brought forth when you have a vision that pulls you toward it. In my business, Nurturing Your Success, the slogan is *"Successful—Think it. Do it. Be it."* This is the formula for success. Visualize what you want first, then start taking necessary action steps to make it happen, and it will become you.

COACHING NOTE: What Is Vision?

"A vision is like a lighthouse which illuminates rather than limits, gives direction rather than destination. Almost all successful individuals and organizations have one thing in common: the power and depth of their vision. A positive, meaningful vision of the future supported by compelling goals provides purpose and direction in the present."

—James J. Mapes, author and hypnotherapist

Vision provides the beacon to keep you focused on what you want to achieve. Without a vision, you're more likely to flounder and drift with the changing times. A vision is a dream, a possibility for the future. A compelling vision excites and motivates you, pulling you toward it. Having a vision draws you closer to it without effort; it pulls you forward rather than you pushing to make something happen.

Write your vision down on paper describing what you see in detail or create a collage of pictures that remind you of what you want and hang it on a wall in clear view. By keeping your vision in front of you, you breathe life into it and with each action you take, each day that goes by, you slowly begin to manifest that vision. Visions aren't realized overnight; they take a long time and persistent attention to cultivate into reality. By having the vision, you ensure a meaningful and purposeful life experience.

Without a life plan or strategy for life success, you get stuck living your life by default. You succumb to the habits you formed perhaps years, even decades ago, at a different time and place. You do what's expected and what you are accustomed to, not taking risks and never asking yourself the important questions about what you really want in your life. When you live like this, you lead a life of mediocrity. You settle for living a life doing less than what you are capable of. You are the only one who can change that.

One of my clients complained of living a mediocre life. Jim identified this after a session we had where he discovered that it was his ambivalence that stood in the way of his moving forward in his life. His ambivalence about life was also affecting his marriage. After a miscarriage a year before, his wife had become depressed. She wanted to have a child. She was 40 years old and "time was running out." Like most things in his life, Jim told her he didn't care one way or the other whether they had children. His ambivalence was distressing to her. She needed him to take her desire to have a child seriously. She needed her feelings to be acknowledged and she needed him to take a stand.

They have since had those important conversations, and as I write this, she is pregnant. He is also completing his master's degree.

When you start asking yourself the tough questions about yourself and how you want to live, you reclaim your power and open the door to the possibilities that life has to offer. Asking yourself the questions about success and what you really want brings it into consciousness. You become aware of the choices you have regarding your life. You begin the journey of accepting responsibility for your life. You stop living by default and start living by design. In essence, you take the driver's seat on the road of your life.

There are many questions that arise in considering your definition of success. And there are several different areas to consider for defining success: personal development, spiritual development, health and your body, relationships, career, and finances. It's often easier if you ask yourself what success will look like and feel like in each of these areas. Will you have lots of money and the things that money can buy? Will you have reached a particular level of status through the position you hold at work? Will a successful life be one that includes being healthy and fit? How will it feel when you are successful? Perhaps success includes living in peace, being connected with your spirituality and having deep, meaningful relationships with others. Perhaps success will be when you are able to creatively use your talents and get paid well for doing what you love to do.

As I travel on my life journey, I often stop to ask myself, "Am I having fun? Is this enjoyable for me?" No longer do I choose to spend time on things that do not bring me satisfaction and joy. I have the opportunity to live successfully every day.

Some people live in a cycle of survival, living paycheck to paycheck, never seeming to get ahead with bills. They may even be digging a hole with credit card debt, living a lifestyle to fulfill some unmet need. Their career is going nowhere. They seem to always find themselves in the same bad relationships. They don't seem to be able to identify the pattern that keeps them repeating this negative cycle. You can succeed at survival, but is survival success?

A Walk Through the Clouds: The Scarcity Mentality

"There is no situation so hopeless, no problem so frightening, no challenge so huge that you couldn't overcome it with proper perspective, heart-felt hope and a sense of purpose. We were not placed on this Earth to just survive. We are here to live life to the fullest and to be happy and prosper. Happiness and prosperity are not only for the special few. They are our birthright. We deserve them."
—John Harricharan, author and lecturer

People who focus only on survival, who believe that there is not enough, that there will never be enough, are functioning under the paradigm of scarcity and lack. Scarcity is an obstacle because it suggests that there are not enough resources and that in order to get what you want you need to fight for it. This implies hard work and competition, meaning that life will be full of struggle and effort.

A different paradigm to consider is one of abundance. Abundance means that there is plenty of what you need—more than enough. When you come from the perspective of abundance, there is lightness; things become less stressful if you know that there is plenty of opportunity—you just need to find it, plenty of time—you just need to learn how to use it wisely, plenty of money—you just need to learn how to value yourself so you can make it and save it, and learn to manage it well. Abundance offers you the opportunity to move beyond survival and into exceptional.

The fact is that you have access to everything you need. Things may not be what you *want* or what you *think* they should be. When you stop fighting what is, you see that where you are right now has richness to it. There is a reason for everything; the universe is not haphazard in its movement. And although you don't want to get caught up in figuring out the "why," you can move forward knowing that there is a reason, an intention, and perhaps it's just not visible or understandable to you right now.

When you shift your perspective to look for what is perfect about your situation, you see other possibilities, that although things may not be as you want them to be, there is something you are meant to learn from the experience. You're right where you're supposed to be. And when you come from this place, you know that whatever you are going through is teaching you something. The growth is in the moment. When you learn to experience the moment, you realize that whatever is happening outside you is not as important as what is going on inside you.

If you are coming from a place of lack, then that's what you'll get: more "lack." When you speak about wanting more, whether it's more money or more patience or more love, what you're really saying is that you don't have enough. What you think about you bring about. Start to identify where you're coming from lack.

If you are coming from a place of abundance and plenty, then you will bring more abundance into your life. Yes, it's the glass half-full/half-empty comparison. And yet, if you expect the glass to always be half-empty, how can it become anything different? If, on the other hand, you believe that the cup runneth over, then the sky is the limit!

COACHING TIP: Adopt an abundance mentality. Abundance is everywhere. Look to nature where abundance can be easily observed: the stars, the blades of grass, the ants, and the rays of the sun. By learning to think and act from a place of abundance, you will see that there is always more available. There is always more waiting for you to discover it.

The Pursuit of Stuff

Years ago, I was having dinner sitting at a bar and the gentleman sitting next to me started up a conversation. It turned out he was one of the richest men in the county where I lived. Although I'd never met him before, I recognized his name when he introduced himself. He was visibly drunk and told me the story of his life: how his beautiful wife had started doing drugs and was having an affair with her drug dealer. He couldn't understand why she would choose that man over himself. He was drinking in hopes of drowning his sorrows.

I was very young at the time and all I could think was that clearly money isn't everything.

How many times do we hear of famous people who use drugs or commit a crime? They seem to have it all: fame, wealth, power, influence, houses, cars—every*thing*, yet they throw it all away. We cannot understand what would make them do something to ruin their lives when they worked so hard to get there in the first place.

The external rewards they obtain from using their talents and abilities are not enough to build character and to develop their personhood. When you are fortunate enough to discover your talents, and you develop your knowledge and skills to become a master, you cannot neglect to develop your Inner Self. There is no running away from yourself. If there are issues from your past that you have not addressed, they will continue to haunt you. If there are fears and self-doubts that you harbor and you never deal with them, they will create a ceiling under which you remain stuck from achieving higher levels of greatness. There is a universal spiritual law that states that if you do not learn the lesson when it presents itself, it will return and return. What we resist persists.

The famous person who neglects his or her Inner Self, who fails to continue to develop personally, will appear to have everything but will remain at the emotional and spiritual level they were before they were famous. *We cannot separate our external reality from our internal reality and expect to live excellent lives.*

If you want to be successful, you must plan for it. A personal evolution must occur so you are prepared for this new level of living. If, for example, you find yourself the recipient of a financial windfall, then you must quickly shift your mentality and beliefs so your inner reality catches up with the external reality.

This is known to happen with lottery players who win millions. Although they become millionaires, they have not made the inner shift to become a rich person. They just suddenly have a lot of money. Once the money is spent, they return to their lives as they were previously. Remnants of the event may be evident in the clothes they wear or the car they drive but little else has changed. Sometimes, people just aren't prepared to handle a financial windfall; they become overwhelmed and are unable to cope appropriately with the added responsibilities.

There is a difference in the way rich people think. If a new lottery winner wants to hold onto that money, he or she must quickly learn to think like a millionaire. The new lottery winner must change his or her thinking, or risk quickly losing his or her new fortune.

A Walk Through the Clouds: Deservingness

Do you believe you deserve a great life? Do you believe you deserve to be happy? To be successful? To be brilliant? To be beautiful? To make lots of money? To have all of your dreams come true?

If you don't, why not?

The fact is that you deserve a great life! You are here, on this earth, living at this time. You have a right to be here and to enjoy everything that the universe has to offer.

COACHING TIP: Stop questioning whether you deserve to receive and experience great things! The ego and your inner critic want you to believe you're unworthy. Your self simply wants to be. Give your best and reap the rewards. If there is someone in your life who might be upset if you were more successful, give yourself permission to be successful anyway! This is your life experience. Do not shrink in order to please anyone else. Regardless of what you do, you can never make someone else happy. Enjoy yourself while you are here. As you do, just like the tree, the world enjoys the fruits of your efforts.

The Internal Rewards

Basing your success on internal rewards instead of external rewards such as cars, vacations, and money, means you are free—free to set your own standards, free from the burden of living someone else's definition of success. When you base success on the internal rewards, those things that make you feel good, it doesn't mean that money doesn't matter. It means that you seek to do your best, be happy, and enjoy what you do. It's the pursuit of happiness rather than status. It's the pursuit of developing your skills and talents to the fullest and in doing so you find prestige and fame. It's in the pursuit of excellence and being the best at what you do and finding that people will pay your fees or salary for your skills and talents. The external rewards become natural byproducts of living a life based on being your personal best.

The fact is you cannot find what you are looking for in something outside of you. You cannot buy enough stuff to make you happy; there will always be a longing for something more.

The inner successes can only come from within you. When you aspire to be great, you do great things, and this translates into deep personal satisfaction as well as external rewards.

Four Areas of Realization

There are four areas that require attention in our lives: mental, physical, spiritual, and emotional. I call them *realizations* because the word "realization" means attention and fulfillment, and ultimately each of us seeks some understanding in and mastery of each area as we strive for "success." To be able to identify these areas and apply some effort, energy, and focus in each area, we maximize the possibility for experiencing a complete life.

Many people focus on one or two areas without spending any or only minimal time on the others. Others lead with one area, meaning there is one area where they are particularly proficient or well versed. There is no judgment here. There is no right or wrong. Knowing that these four areas of realization exist can help you identify areas of learning or growth that perhaps will bring you greater joy and personal fulfillment.

The Mind

The mental realm is where we conquer the mind. We think. We learn. We use our mental faculties in order to produce and create. This is a good thing. But it is not the *only* thing. Many people pursue the mind without attention to the other areas of realization and by doing so limit the extent of their achievement. Without consideration of those things beyond the mind's understanding, there is a ceiling under which the most intelligent of men and women will remain. There is a knowing and intelligence that exists outside of the mind.

To understand and learn how to maximize your mind is part of your life experience. Understanding how you learn and how your mind works is essential for you to be successful. Notice how the mind protects itself when you try to change a habit or question a long-held belief. Your ego lets you know when something is changing. It loves the status quo. Learning to be more conscious of how your mind works is an important part of the self-discovery process. Simply pay attention. The more you notice, the more you can learn to honor your mind to maximize its abilities for greater impact.

For years I focused on being an intellectual. I was always analyzing and thinking and learning. As a child, friends used to tell me, "You 'think' too much." But I enjoy contemplation, intellectual stimulation, and analysis.

I completed several degrees; my family thought I'd be in school forever! They called me a professional student. During those years, I was committed to filling my brain with information that I enjoyed learning about. When I had completed my master's degree, I didn't want to pursue additional degrees at the time. I wanted to learn how to use the knowledge I'd accumulated over the years to make a difference in the world. I wanted to see what I could do with it all. I made the inner shift from student to professional. And although I'll always be open to learning new things, by acknowledging myself as a professional, I accept that I'm enough, that I know enough, and that I can make a great recipe with the ingredients I already have. This is a huge distinction because there is a different identity, a different "sense of self" when you still consider yourself a novice, new, or "not enough" versus seeing yourself as a practitioner, as someone proficient and accomplished at something.

Although I am dedicated to lifelong learning and I continue to learn every day, it's not necessarily from a book or from a course. I am a true student of life. A big part of my learning is simply from paying attention to what is, to what is happening within me, and to what thoughts my mind creates. Although I still read a lot of books and seek more information, I know that feeding the mind is not enough. It's only one part of what life is all about.

You can certainly continue to add more and more education to your mind, but it will not make you feel successful without learning to use the knowledge you gain. There will always be a longing for more knowledge, more understanding, and more information. But it's not enough to *have* knowledge. The power of knowledge is in the *use* of it.

There is a huge gap that exists between education and application. There are many people who remain stuck either in learning mode not realizing the value of the knowledge they already have, or in not knowing how to apply the knowledge they have in a way that's meaningful for them. Learning to explore within, to begin *The Journey Called YOU*, is a great place to start. The answers may not come through the mind, but rather may be called forth from another area of realization. Learn to quiet the mind and make space for other forms of intelligence.

"We should take care not to make the intellect our god; it has, of course, powerful muscles, but no personality. It cannot lead; it can only serve."
—Albert Einstein

Physical Environment

The physical realm is where form exists. This is where your body and material things are accumulated and understood. Each of us must deal with the shape of our bodies and we need to find a way to make money that affords us a lifestyle that we enjoy. Every "thing" that exists is part of this realm. This is not, however, all there is—although this is the area where everything can be seen and touched. This is where we witness the manifestation of our labors. This is the area of "what."

The intellect and the physical realizations are where most people play. They use their minds, also a part of the physical realm, and receive rewards in the physical realm. While all four of the realizations work best in concert, this area is often the most celebrated because the physical realm is what people can see and touch. Creating an ideal body is physical but it's also spiritual since the body is your spirit's house and by taking good care of your body, you are honoring yourself. There is a level of mastery to be achieved in this area including learning to maximize the mind-body connection and using the body as a vehicle for sensing your feelings and emotional energy, as well as accessing your intuition.

Focusing on only the physical part of your body and how your body looks can become an obsession and like anything, you can place too much emphasis in this area of the physical realm.

The same can be said for making money and the accumulation of stuff. There are many wonderful "things" to try and to enjoy in the world; often people become too attached to their stuff, mistakenly think-ing that having more stuff is the path to fulfillment. Being a spender rather than a saver, for instance, and spending every dollar that comes into your possession is evidence of that "longing for something more but looking in the wrong place." Perhaps what you seek cannot be found in the physical realm. You cannot find yourself there. There are reli-gious sects and individuals who denounce the material part of this area in search of more meaning and a deeper connection to the nonform.

Learning balance and how to play in this area while also learning and discovering in the other realizations, will help you maintain an appropriate detachment to your "stuff." As long as you enjoy your stuff, wonderful. But the moment it becomes a burden, or it no longer brings you joy, get rid of it. Someone somewhere is looking for the very thing you no longer want. By learning to let go of stuff, you continually cre-ate space for new and wonderful things to enjoy. You cannot find security in having lots of stuff, although many people try; just like security can-not be found in a job or in a spouse, it will not be found in having lots of stuff. Security is illusionary. The security you seek is in your under-standing of the universe and in becoming comfortable with the temporary nature of life.

Spiritual Intelligence

Spiritual intelligence is the understanding of that which has no form. It's the understanding of the laws of the universe and how the universe operates. Many people mistake religion for spirituality. Reli-gion is a path that often leads to spirituality; it is not the same as spirituality.

Going to church, synagogue, or temple once a week; reading the prayers; asking for forgiveness; and celebrating holidays are the prac-tices of religious people (the form) that are different from spirituality (the nonform). These acts can bring someone to a spiritual place. But spirituality transcends religion. It exists in all religions. It's like taking a different route to get to the same destination. It really doesn't matter which route you take; we all end up in the same place *if* we are seeking the Truth of the universe. What matters most is whether your religion brings you the answers you seek and whether the traditions, prayers, and celebrations are those that you enjoy. If you do not feel good when you participate in your religion, then investigate others. Settling for something that doesn't bring you joy is no longer an option.

Each of us is on a journey of the spirit. Life is spirit brought into form (physical); so each of us is on a spiritual as well as a physical journey. The challenge of life is to integrate your physical body with your spirit so they move effortlessly through this experience. Have you ever met someone whose spirit just simply didn't seem to do well in their body? I cannot explain it any other way. Perhaps this is where some mental illnesses come in; people just can't seem to handle this world.

Although clearly there are numerous questions that can be raised, caution must be taken when exploring the "why" questions of the universe. You can easily become frustrated by not having the answers. The universe will let you know the answers when it's time and the answers will not come through the mind. The answers come to you through your access to the collective consciousness that exists beyond the mind. The collective consciousness—all that is known—is the Divine and your access to it is called intuition.

> **"The intellect has little to do on the road to discovery. There comes a leap in consciousness, call it intuition or what you will, and the solution comes to you and you don't know how or why."**
> —Albert Einstein

Emotional Intelligence

This brings us to the fourth realization of life, the emotional realm. Not only does emotional intelligence exist, but also our ability to *access* the knowing that exists in our bodies. Our bodies store emotional energy. This energy is knowledge. It cannot be accessed by the mind; however, it can be understood by the mind once experienced by the body.

> **"There can be no knowledge without emotion. We may be aware of a truth, yet until we have felt its force, it is not ours. To the cognition of the brain must be added the experience of the soul."**
> —Arnold Bennett, British author

Understanding that life is not made up of any one area of mastery but rather has several areas of intelligence and focus, it's easy to see how a person who is stuck in any one area is limiting him- or herself.

If you're not content with something in life, or if there is a longing for deeper understanding or a feeling that something is missing, honor it by exploring these four realms. Your discontent is a way *in*; it's an opportunity for you to ask questions of yourself and of how you are living. When you understand which dimension you're living in and leading with, you realize how you're limiting yourself and you can choose to develop your intelligence in a different realization. The more aware you are about *who you are*, about what feels good for you, and the more you make choices that honor you, the higher the quality of your life.

Judy and her husband had been married for seven years when she became a client. She was looking to change her career. Whenever questions were raised about her husband or their relationship in our sessions, Judy wouldn't go there. "Everything is fine," was her reply.

Recently, they bought a new home, something out of a magazine—it was beautiful. They had talked about buying a bigger house for years and finally decided this is what they needed to really make them happy. They added a porch and were putting in a sunroom when Judy began to feel stuck. She realized that she had everything she wanted yet it was tremendously unsatisfying and she couldn't understand why.

One day, Judy met a friend who invited her home for a family dinner where she discovered a simple home, nothing fancy or elaborate, but it was filled with warmth and love. What she thought she wanted looked good to the world but it didn't *feel good* in her heart. It was at this moment she realized that regardless of logic, regardless of what other people said or thought, and regardless of the "looks of things," she wasn't *in joy* in her beautiful new house. It wasn't what she wanted. It wasn't what she was searching for. What she *really* wanted was to *feel* good rather than *look* good. Her house was just a building with four walls and she wasn't happy in her marriage. Judy made the connection between the different realizations, how her pursuit of "stuff" wasn't enough of what she truly wanted, and therefore, it didn't make her happy. Instead of leading her life looking for the physical, she could learn to lead with the emotional realm, what "feels good" or feels right to her, and by doing so, fill her life with joy. This was more about what success looked like and felt like for Judy. In order to create a life of joy, she first needed to eliminate those things that stood in the way of her happiness. Judy decided to divorce her husband, they sold their house, and she's now charting a new course for success.

Balancing the four realizations is essential. When any one area blocks the others, the results are often not what you want. When you fall in love, for instance, the emotions become overwhelming and block out your ability to reason, which is not a good thing. It feels great but you can easily do things that are not in your best interest. The same is true when you are overwhelmed by other emotions such as shame, anger, or guilt.

When you are unable to manage your emotions, what you may find is that your needs become more evident. When you fall in love, for instance, your needs for attention, affection, or to be needed may come out full force. What happens then, is that your needs meet your potential partner's needs and the two bond. The needs are matched, but this is not love. If you learn how to manage your emotions and keep your head in the game, you can identify your needs and get them met in a healthy way without flooding this new potential mate and either scaring him or her away or bonding with his or her needs. It's all about balance and being fully present to what is.

Setting Your Course

If you look at each of the different physical areas of your life—finances, romantic relationship, family, friends, community, career, home, equipment—which do you feel good about? In what ways are you already successful? Besides having lots of money, there are many other ways to be successful. You may have an abundance of opportunities where you may use your skills and talents. You may have a wonderful intimate relationship, good friends, strong ties with family and your community. You may love your home and live in the geographic area you love. Perhaps you enjoy your work yet you lack balance; more balance would bring you success. You may be in excellent health and in that way you are successful.

As you take the time to evaluate your life, you will find areas you wish to improve. These are the areas where you set goals for the future. The voids are where you invest your time and energy to improve your level of enjoyment. For each area, ask yourself what success would look like, feel like, and how you would be different. What would success look like if money were flowing into your life? What would a fabulous relationship with your spouse be like?

I asked Yvonne that and she was speechless. She had never considered that her twenty-three-year marriage could be "fabulous." She never knew anyone who had a fantastic marriage. She stated, "You just learn to put up with it. That's what my mother did. That's what I see other people do."

Without considering that it could be different, she never thought to change it. And without a vision for what she believed was a successful marriage, success in marriage meant you just stay together forever and put up with whatever you got. She never thought about their quality of life and how their marriage could be molded into something wonderful.

Marriage is a partnership where each person shares the best of him/ herself and asks that of the other. But it requires effort, attention, a vision for success, and patience. You have to hold that place of greatness for your partner and ask them to hold the same place for you.

With this new frame of reference, however, Yvonne could now create a vision for a successful marriage, discuss this with her husband, and together they can work to make the vision their reality. It's like starting over. How exciting for them!

When you define success, ask yourself what it feels like to achieve it. If success is about *who you are becoming*, freeing yourself from living by other people's standards, accepting responsibility for your success by continuing to stretch your capabilities, and living in truth about who you are, then how will you know you are succeeding? What benchmarks will you set to determine your progress?

"Success is not a doorway, it's a staircase."
—Dottie Walters, author

Success isn't something you get and you're done. It's a journey. With each level of success you achieve, you'll discover there's another level to climb. It really is like a staircase. There's always something to wonder about, another puzzle of you to discover, and another area or a deeper level of realization to explore and understand. As you realize some level of success in a particular area of life, you'll be inspired with a new and bigger vision.

Personal development and creating your best self are at the heart of living a successful life. Personal development is a lifelong process. External rewards will increase at the rate at which you evolve and become more of who you are. Your success is limited to the extent at which you limit yourself. If you want something different in your life, you must become different. Only you have the power to release yourself from the bondages of self. It's not something that can be given to you, but you *can* learn to get out of your own way.

A Walk Through the Clouds: Getting Out of Your Own Way

"Most of the shadows of this life are caused by standing in one's own sunshine."
—Ralph Waldo Emerson

What does it mean to get out of your own way? It means that you often stand in the way of your achieving the very things you say you want. This can show up in your life in a number of ways such as lack of knowledge, lack of commitment, your inner critic, sabotage, excuses, rationalizing—any of the obstacles (or clouds) in this book. By holding yourself back, you limit your success.

Kim is a client who had never put herself first and had a very difficult time loving and accepting herself. Learning this through our work together was extremely difficult for her. She is accustomed to putting everyone's needs before her own. Now that her kids are grown, it's harder for her to hide in caring for others; she cannot deny her desires and needs any longer. As long as she continues to believe that she is second rate, she will not be able to move beyond the level on which she currently operates. She cannot move up the staircase of success.

There needs to be a level of preparedness to take the next step, a willingness to shed your attachment to *what was* and an openness to be with *what is*. By being unwilling to see herself as deserving of her own love and attention, Kim limits her level of enjoyment and peace, meaning her life is not as great as she knows it could be. Creating this shift is a process that will take time and a new perspective. Kim needs to learn to be good to herself and patient with herself.

How do you get out of your own way? By paying attention to how you're standing *in* your own way and focusing on what you want to have happen rather than on the obstacles. Awareness gives you power.

COACHING TIP: What you think about, you bring about. Focus on the outcome you desire. Let nothing—even you—get in the way of your achieving the desired results. If something appears to impede your progress, deal with it immediately and completely. Anything you see as an obstacle is truly an opportunity to explore, learn, and grow. A coach can help you learn how to get out of your own way so if you're having difficulty with this, consider hiring a coach to work with you. Don't let anything or anyone stand in your way of living a great life—even you!

The Inner Shift

An inner shift is a change in the way you think, believe, or feel about something. It is adopting a new perspective—a new paradigm. Once you think differently about something, you naturally change your behavior. You become someone new. Adopting a new perspective makes all the difference in the world when it comes to the successful achievement of any goal you desire.

Most people try to change their behavior. This may work for a while but it is rarely sustainable. *Who you are* is an important part of the equation toward achieving what you want. Your thoughts and paradigms drive your actions, which bring about the results you achieve. If you focus on the thoughts, perspectives, and beliefs that govern your behavior, you will naturally change how you act in order to produce different outcomes. Change how you think, change how you think about yourself, and you easily change the results in your life.

Whatever achievement or success you experience, *you* change in the process. If you get a new promotion or complete a degree, you become someone new as you step into this new reality. Learn to change your identity in order to prepare yourself for success and you are more likely to achieve what you want and with much less effort and struggle. Visualization can help you see *who you need to be* in order to be prepared for whatever it is you seek. This is referred to as an *inner shift*.

Many people have tried to quit smoking to no avail. They try every tool available but nothing seems to work. Before you ever put down the cigarette, you must redefine yourself and become a nonsmoker. This is where the work is. You must change your identity. It can take weeks, even months, of internal dialogue to reprogram you from a smoker to a nonsmoker. You must repeatedly tell yourself that you are a nonsmoker. You must define what that means for you. What will change in your life? What do nonsmokers do or not do that you need to learn? Will you dress differently? What will be different in your home and car? Will you spend time with different people? Will you need to change where you spend your time? What will you do with the extra money that you will have? How will you take breaks during the day if you're not taking smoke breaks? There are many questions you must ask yourself and answer completely.

Once you get clear about who you are *in your mind* as a nonsmoker, you gradually start doing things differently. You might start sitting in the nonsmoking section in restaurants. You might clear out your car and your home and no longer permit any smoking in these areas. Each small step you take moves you toward becoming a nonsmoker. Then, one day you wake up and you simply don't smoke. The last thing you do is put down the cigarettes because nonsmokers don't smoke.

(In case you are wondering, this is how I quit smoking in 1994 after smoking a pack a day for sixteen years. It was easy once I did the inner work, and I've never looked back.)

There is no stress about "quitting smoking" because that is not your goal. Your goal is to become a nonsmoker. By making an inner shift, you become someone new and eventually take the actions necessary to achieve the mind's understanding of *who you are*. Change how you think about who you are and your actions will follow, creating the results you want.

Other addictions are a bit different in that people must abstain from using their drug of choice before they can change who they are. Drugs impair one's thinking. Once their bodies and minds are freed from their physical addictions and they learn to just stay clean one day at a time, then they can rescript their internal messages and learn to know themselves, accept themselves, and be kind to themselves. Drug and alcohol abuse is always a symptom of a deeper problem and requires professional assistance. People abuse themselves either to hide from their emotional pain or because they haven't yet learned how to accept their greatness and love themselves. Eventually, the drug may take over and they become physically and psychologically addicted. Once clean, they need to learn to accept and love themselves. This is not always an easy prescription but it's the only way to overcome the life of self-bondage.

Weight loss is another charged topic. Similar to the process of becoming a nonsmoker, you need to determine what it looks and feels like to be a smaller size and weight. Don't start with the goal of losing a certain amount of weight. You don't want to focus on *losing* anything. When you lose something, what's the first thing you do? You look for it! You want to focus on gaining something—strength, endurance, tone, health, or fitness.

Weight loss is the "what." Make a shift in how you think about your weight and your body. Learn to love and marvel at your body. Make a shift in your relationship with food. Pay attention to what food means to you. Food is a source of pleasure and to this end, people tend to abuse it. If, instead, you think of food as fuel or as an energy source for your body, you will naturally eat differently. Start paying attention to what you eat, how much you're eating, when you're eating, what you're eating for (hunger, pleasure, something to do, and so forth), and how it makes you feel. The more present you are, you may discover that most of the time you're not even enjoying your food because you're busy doing or thinking about something else. You look down, the plate is empty, and you're wondering who ate your food and how you got to be so full!

Carve out time for eating and be mindful of how your body feels when you eat different foods. You've been given this incredible body; honor it and learn how to give it the fuel it needs to work best for you. Eating is a pleasurable activity but it's not the only way to experience pleasure throughout the course of your day. Food provides your body with energy. If you're eating the wrong foods, eating more than your body needs, and not getting enough exercise, it's easy to understand how you're gaining weight. And if you're not present while eating, you're not even receiving pleasure but rather you're eating on autopilot. Eating has become habit.

Visualize yourself healthy and trim. Who are you when you dream of being healthy? How do you care for your body that is different from how you treat your body now? What are you doing differently in this vision of health? Perhaps you weigh a certain amount or fit into a certain size of clothing. You might envision how you will feel, how you will carry yourself differently, and how much more confident you are.

When you shift the focus to creating a lifestyle based on being healthy, what are some things you will change? You would include structured exercise because that is healthy. You might drink more water, add some new foods and eliminate some unhealthy foods. You might read about nutrition or meet with a nutritionist to learn more about the foods that work best for your body. You might become more active, slowly introducing new activities into your life that get you off the couch and away from the television. You might seek out a new community of friends to support your new, healthy lifestyle. You'll also want to add other pleasurable activities; if you're doing lots of things that bring you joy, you won't use food to fill a need. It'll just be used for fuel, which means you'll eat less, and if you learn to be fully present while eating—meaning you do nothing else but focus on the pleasure of eating—then you'll truly enjoy it.

Write out your vision for how you want your body to look and feel. If you have a clear vision, that vision will pull you forward and you'll start choosing behaviors that will honor your vision for success. And by creating a lifestyle around being healthy, you'll find your relationships will change—with others, with yourself, with food, and with your body.

Shedding the pounds is a byproduct of treating your body well and of truly loving your body—this place you call "home." The fat comes off because your body no longer needs to store the excess energy and you are no longer giving it excess to store. This is not the only outcome. By envisioning a healthy body, you can discover other outcomes you desire. Perhaps you want to play in a sport or try a new activity. By seeking out other physical ways to add pleasure, you may discover other activities you would enjoy, such as dancing or learning to play an instrument.

Like anything, health is a journey and there will be levels of success for you to achieve, benchmarks that allow for celebration, and new visions for success. There is no quick fix. There is no weight-loss gimmick that will give you the sustained success you seek. It may provide you with some returns but they will be short-lived. This has been proven time and time again. This isn't *Star Trek*; you cannot ask Scottie to beam you into the perfect body. You have to create it. You have to learn to love the body you've been given for your life experience—every part of it—scars, bulges, and all. Once you make the inner shift to change your perspective, you start making consistent, deliberate changes in your behavior, which over time takes you from where you are to where you want to be.

A Walk Through the Clouds: The Quick Fix

"Brilliance is an after-the-fact perception created by success. There's no fast path, no magic formula. It's all hard work and perseverance."
—Steve Mills of IBM

Everybody wants things to happen quickly. Once you make a decision to change something, you want it now. Making the decision was challenging enough, now you want results.

This way of thinking is a trap. It detours you away from doing the necessary inner work and focuses you on taking shortcuts, which inevitably end up being "long" cuts.

Things don't happen overnight. The universe doesn't work that way. Understand that once you change what you are committed to—once you shift to become a different you—the universe will support you, but it does so in its own time. Learning to understand the way of the universe is another level of awareness.

COACHING TIP: There are three things to make note of here. One: Accept where you are right now on your journey. Two: Learn to look at the bigger picture over time (your lifetime). And three: Examine your relationship with time. Time is your friend. In creating a great life, it's not a destination. You don't arrive there; you experience it. It's happening now. It's a journey. Learn to enjoy the ride!

Whether the area you're working on is your body, your community, your family, your career or business, your spiritual understanding or religious involvement, finding a life partner, your finances, your children, your relationship with your spouse, your friends, and so on, success takes time. The people you see who are highly successful spent years working up to where you see them today. It's easy to look at someone and say, "They had it easy. They were lucky. They had opportunities I didn't have." The fact is it took a lot of hard work to move them to where they are. The climb is always challenging and it always takes time. It takes time to make the inner shift and then it takes time to manifest the results. And, until you're ready to make that inner shift, to do the necessary inner work, your external work will be in vain. Chart your course for success by envisioning what you want and then asking yourself who you need to become in order to achieve that. And then, just keep moving forward.

The Path to Success
"Successful—Think it. Do it. Be it."

The path to success starts with a vision—what do you want? The vision is for something different in the future. As you "see" the vision of "what" you want more clearly, identify yourself in the vision. *Who are you* in this future reality? How are you different? Who do you need to become in order to achieve what you want? This is the inner work that needs to be done.

Start making the necessary inner shifts to become this new person you'll need to evolve into in order to prepare yourself for the success you will achieve. The inner work comes first. How will your new reality feel? What will be different about you? What learning needs to take place in order for you to be at that point in the future? Take a realistic assessment for how long the inner work will take. It takes longer than you think, depending on what obstacles—or clouds—are in your way and need to be walked through.

Then, as you start feeling different about *who you are*, look outside yourself to start changing your surroundings to fit your new reality. This, too, takes time. Start by eliminating the things that do not serve you in your vision. Start designing an environment that will support and nurture you on your new path. With each new day, you have a new opportunity to move another step closer to your dream. And with each movement you make toward your new reality, the path becomes clearer. With clarity, the universe has a way of giving us exactly what we need in order to fulfill our dream. Gifts, people, teachers, and tools all enter your path to aid you on your course. Everything you need to achieve what you want is accessible; you simply need to get on the path and start preparing you—which is exactly what you have control over. Let the universe do its work by trusting that if you do your part, the tools you need will be provided. This is where the magic comes in. You have to trust and have faith…

Each day that goes by offers you an opportunity to celebrate the changes you're making and to examine your mistakes, making the necessary adjustments to put you back on path. As the months go by, you can look at how far you've come down your path and you can look ahead at where you are going and you'll *know* you're traveling the right road for you. And as you evolve and your vision is achieved, you'll create new visions, new environments, and become more of *who you are capable of becoming*. It's a journey—your *life* journey.

Here is your formula for success:
Vision + Inner Work + New Environment + Action + Time = Success

In the next chapter, we discuss time in more detail—your relationship with time and how you can learn to spend more time doing the things that you love, that maximize *who you are*. But first, a brief interlude.

Coaching Challenge

- Write in your journal about success. What does success mean to you?

- How will you know when you are successful? What benchmarks will let you know that you are living successfully? How will it feel?

- What changes are you struggling to make right now in your life? What would it be like to surrender to the fact that you're just not ready? What if you gave yourself permission to give up the fight and acknowledge that right now you're not ready and instead, focus on doing the inner work?

- What three goals do you want to achieve this year? Who will you need to become in order to achieve those goals?

A Story From The Journey Called ME

"Our own life is the instrument with which we experiment with the truth."
—Thich Nhat Hanh, Vietnamese Buddhist monk

It was June 2001 and I had just completed the requirements for my master's degree in business. I was excited to be finished. As a single mother, completing graduate school while working full-time was challenging. After three years of juggling babysitters and having no social life, I was looking forward to a reprieve from structured education. At the same time, I was concerned. I thought I would miss the intellectual challenge and stimulation found in my graduate classes. What I wanted was to build my life around my desire to learn. I wondered how I could have stimulating and provocative conversations each day. I value learning and expansive thinking. This is a "piece" of who I am. But my jobs up until this point had been mostly tactical in nature, meaning I performed lots of tasks rather than doing a lot of thinking.

With graduate school behind me, I began to reevaluate my situation at work. I was ready for an increase in responsibility, an opportunity to advance so I could use my skills. I began to question what was next for me. And then, I had a push.

One week after completing my master's degree, the company where I worked reengineered the human resources department and our positions were eliminated. This was a huge loss for me: a single mom suddenly

93

without a means to support her family, certainly a scary place for anyone to find herself.

But I had a different perspective. The perspective I chose to take was to treat this as an opportunity to explore the possibilities for me. It's strange to admit this, but I was excited. I felt really blessed. It seems strange that someone would actually be glad to lose her job, but I was. I knew that I was ready for something more—there was a yearning inside me—and this company didn't have an opportunity for me. I received three months' severance and used the time to find other employment. This was a good thing!

As a matter of fact, this was my third layoff in a row. If I were the type of person to take things personally, this would have really damaged my self-esteem. Layoffs are business decisions; they're not personal, even if it feels that way. In this case, the department was eliminated; it wasn't about me. They had no use for someone with my education and I had grown beyond the capacity of my current position.

I thought, "Here I go again," and began the arduous task of job hunting, something I knew well but did not enjoy. It was summertime, a perfect time to be out of work. But as a single parent, I was nervous about being out of work for long. I treated the job hunt as a job in itself. I spent regular working hours seeking other employment, scouring the papers and the online job boards. I sent out letters to area businesses introducing myself. I had numerous interviews both in person and by phone.

The offers started to come in. But there was this yearning inside me. I couldn't explain it but there was this very strong feeling not to take any of these offers. It was as if every fiber of my being was crying out to me. Clearly, my spirit was trying to get my attention. I just wasn't sure what it was trying to say! I was becoming frustrated; like most people, I needed an income. I had to work. I'm not independently wealthy. (Not yet, anyway!)

Although I had been involved in two other layoffs, this time was different. Previously, one company had closed and the other job was temporary. In this most recent job, I had been a corporate recruiter. It was a fairly new company when I started and the position was new. I spent two years working very hard to build my position. I put in long hours and produced excellent results. But I had received nothing for my job well done. There was no "thank you," no recognition, and no reward for my work. I felt as though I was undervalued and overworked, and for all my hard work, I was dismissed. My initial feelings were of powerlessness, that I had no control over these events, that I was a victim of circumstances.

The problem with this thinking was that I didn't like feeling powerless! This feeling lit a fire in me. I was determined to figure out why my life was not proceeding in the way I thought it should. We're not powerless. In fact, I believe we do have power, more power than we know how to use. No, I believed that there was a reason this was happening to me and I was committed to learning this lesson so I could reclaim my power. Blaming others or making excuses for the circumstances in my life was not my style.

Nelson Mandela's inaugural speech in 1994 included a passage from Marianne Williamson's book *A Return to Love*. I cut out the passage and hung it on the wall near my desk. It still hangs there today.

> **"Our fear is not that we are inadequate.**
> **Our fear is that we are powerful beyond measure.**
> **It is our light, not our darkness, that most frightens us.**
> **We ask ourselves, who am I to be brilliant, gorgeous, talented, and fabulous? Actually, who are you not to be?**
> **You are a child of God.**
> **Your playing small does not serve the world.**
> **There is nothing enlightened about shrinking so that other people won't feel insecure around you.**
> **We are born to make manifest the glory of God that is within us.**
> **It's not just in some of us; it is in everyone.**
> **And as we let our own light shine, we unconsciously give other people permission to do the same.**
> **As we are liberated from our own fear, our presence automatically liberates others."**

Over the years, I've seen this passage quoted many times but always regarding fears and overcoming our fears about the greatness within us.

I believe that many people do fear their own power. But I wasn't afraid of my power; I just wanted to know *how* I was powerful!

The concept of personal power has always fascinated me. I studied it as part of my graduate school program. Nothing I read, however, gave me the prescription for *finding* this power. I always believed that I could be so much more, that I have so much more to contribute to the world if I only knew how to access this power!

If I am so powerful, I wanted someone to point me in the right direction because I certainly didn't feel very powerful! Three layoffs, divorced, and having experienced some of the worst bosses in the world, I was grasping at anything that might lead me to find my power because, you know, I felt like I was missing the secret. My life was messy and I didn't really know how to be happy.

Hard as it was to admit, I realized that *I* was responsible for my current predicament. Something *I* was doing was causing these results in my life. And if I wanted different results, I had to start doing things differently. But where do I start?

I started by asking myself some serious questions. I decided to take some time off from job hunting since I had no idea where I was headed, and instead spend time getting to know myself. I began journaling every day. I focused my writing on my previous positions and my education, things that stood out in my life as meaningful in some way. I needed to get to know myself at a deeper level. I started asking questions about *who I was* rather than *what* I wanted to do. What brought out the best in me? What did I have to offer the world? Where were my talents, strengths, and skills? What were my likes and dislikes? I had just finished thirteen years of higher education; how was I going to use all of that knowledge and education? What was the impact I would make in the world? What was I meant to do?

As I pondered these questions, I realized that one of the beliefs I learned in my youth was that security rests in having a job. You went to work and in return received a paycheck and some benefits. Clearly, I had found no security in my jobs. I came to realize that security was in my ability to earn a living. It lies within *me*. Security is not found in a job but rather with my ability to make money from using my knowledge, talents, abilities, and skills. Money was merely the exchange of value for my time and energy. The more valuable my time and energy, the more I would make so long as I knew how to best use the package that was Me. This shift in thinking opened the doors for new possibilities about what work could look like.

I questioned my definition of success. Honestly, I had never thought to question it before now. It never occurred to me that I needed to define it. This belief was also set when I was a little girl. I believed that if I found a good company and worked hard, then I would receive raises and promotions and I'd rise to the top. (I never bothered to ask myself whether I *wanted* to be at the top.) This was how it had been for my father. He worked for the same hospital as the chief radiologist for over two decades until they closed, and he was forced into retirement. But was that success? To him, during those times, maybe it was. I had pursued an education to ensure my success. But success, as it was defined for me as a child, was not happening for me. I was not traveling down a path that was bringing me promotions, raises, recognition, and job security. In fact, by this definition, I was failing miserably.

When I took the time to consider success and what it meant to be successful, I realized that the definition I grew up with didn't work for me. In fact, using that definition, success did not include happiness. It only included having a job and other external rewards to be determined by others. My success was in the hands of others and that didn't make sense to me.

When I decided to become a nurse, I had just completed my first bachelor's degree, which was in business. I knew I wanted to be of service, to make a difference in the lives of others. Given the experiences of my past, I was drawn to psychiatric nursing and I really enjoyed helping people in this way. During the 1990s, the United States was in a recession. Jobs were tight. One year, I received a thirteen-cent-an-hour raise. (That was something to run to the bank with!) After that, I went three consecutive years without a raise. Then, the facility went bankrupt and the new owners cut wages by 10 percent. Needless to say, I did not remain at that facility. People who choose the human services industries know full well that they won't become millionaires in these positions. But that was getting ridiculous.

I then moved into human resources, first in a staff development position and then into recruiting. And what happened? Three layoffs in a row. I was getting nowhere.

Or was I?

I was producing successful results in these positions. As a recruiter, for example, I successfully managed to fill nearly three hundred positions within a one-year period. Clearly, this was successful job performance. And as a nurse, I regularly made a difference in the patients I worked with.

I was able to perform the jobs well but that was not enough to move me to where I *thought* I was supposed to go—a promotion, recognition, financial rewards. The questions now became, "Where do I want to go?" "What is important to me?" I had felt for some time that I was not living up to my potential. I felt like I was not following the right path, that I was on the wrong road and unsure of my destination. I needed to identify a vision for my life so I could chart a different course.

First, I needed to know how I defined success. If I knew what success was, then I would know when I had achieved it. I was on a mission. I studied and read about success. I read about successful people and what made them successful. What I realized was that I felt successful when I was learning and growing and using that knowledge to help others to learn and grow. What I realized was that success had less to do with what I received but rather who I was becoming, what I was learning, and how I was able to impact the lives of others.

My paradigm, or way of thinking about success, was really related to how well I performed the work and how much I learned along the way. It was an internal experience. In other words, success was defined by my personal development, my ability to express who I am, and how I feel about the work I'm doing, rather than the external rewards that one might hope to receive.

If I am experiencing life fully every day; if I am adding value in the lives of others through my knowledge and experience; and if I am learning and growing in the process, then I am successful. I want to fully enjoy every moment that I have been blessed with and maximize my time here on this earth. I want to squeeze every drop of potential from me. Happiness and the beauty of life are found in the small, everyday wonders—if we stop long enough to pay attention.

Through this period of self-reflection, I identified my values and priorities and realized that to be truly successful required my living a life that expressed those values. Those values are *who I am*. To deny my values was to deny myself. Success, therefore, flows naturally from living in congruence with my values and living my personal best.

People don't find happiness in doing those things that are incongruent with their values; there will always be a longing and a sense that something is missing. Without using your values as a guide for how to live, it's easy to be distracted by the busyness of life. Try as you might, you will never be satisfied filling your life with things that take you away from who you are at the core. If you're filling your life with the wrong things, you will never find happiness and you will never be truly successful.

When you align yourself with *who you are*, when you live your life in a way that reflects your priorities, when you open the door to all that you can be, then you truly live. Inner peace and personal fulfillment are the rewards for living your values and maximizing your potential. Living authentically, in tune with who you really are, enables you to form deeper relationships. When you live in harmony with who you are meant to be, with what makes you truly happy, the result is that you experience a meaningful and joyful life.

We each have talents and gifts uniquely our own. It's our job—our duty, to discover those gifts and share them with the world. Therein lies our greatness. I knew there was something missing. I knew there was more to life—more to Me, than just working a job and getting a paycheck.

Taking the time to think about my life and what made for success, I considered what made each of my previous positions rewarding. I was looking for a common thread or pattern to my life. What was it about those jobs that made me feel that I mattered in the lives of others? Where did I have the most fun?

Through self-reflection, I identified my primary value as fully expressing myself for all that I can be in order to make a difference in the lives of others. I enjoy working with others—with *you*—so you can feel good about yourself. I want to inspire you to be all that you are capable of becoming, to empower you to access your inner strength and power, and to help eliminate the blocks to living a healthy and happy life. I am also a lifelong learner with a passion for using language and communicating. Translating all of this into something where I could support myself financially was the challenge.

Often, it's difficult to see yourself unobstructed so I looked to others to help me see myself more clearly. Often our talents are right under our nose so we cannot see them. Talents come natural to us so we believe them to be easy and don't give them much thought or attention until others point out how difficult that is for them to do. We also cannot possibly know what we mean in the lives of others unless they share that with us.

First, I considered all of the compliments I had heard over the years from patients, coworkers, bosses, friends, family, and even the interviewees I met as a recruiter. I also spoke to people close to me, family and friends, asking them to share with me what difference I make in their lives and what they would like to see me do. I looked to their wisdom. Their feedback was extremely interesting. When I took the time to ask others for feedback about Me, it gave me insight into what they believed my value was and the contribution I made in their lives. From their comments I learned a bit about how the world received me and this opened my mind to the possibilities of where I needed to change course in my life.

Shortly thereafter, I stumbled upon the coaching profession and knew instantly that this was where I belonged. Not only could I coach, but I could assist others through my writing and public speaking as well. It also meant I could have my own business and be my own boss. I'd also need to be very well-learned in the field (lifelong learning required!).

When I started my personal and professional development company, it was as if everything—all the "secrets"—were suddenly revealed. It wasn't about opening the business, but rather aligning myself with the true purpose of my life and getting on the path toward authenticity. The clarity was incredible; it was as though someone turned on a light bulb into understanding the universe and how things worked. When I became clearer about who I was and what my gifts were (discovering the pieces of my puzzle), it became clearer as to how I might use those gifts to express my values (the picture in the puzzle). I also needed to eliminate the clutter in my way of thinking and the limiting beliefs that had guided my path for so long. By doing this, I could see through the clouds and find my way—my purpose—the path that the universe has in store for me in this lifetime.

Clearly, there are certain elements of power that we can use to design a life that brings us the most joy and meaning. These powers include accepting personal responsibility, increasing our level of awareness, and making choices that honor us. These are key areas of personal power accessible to each of us. Throughout this book, you're learning ways to access and make the most of your own power. The other personal power that is imperative to personal happiness and fulfillment is the ability to communicate effectively, both with others and with you. Accessing your power is about mastering yourself and it all starts with becoming more aware and your willingness to "see" more deeply into what is.

When I freed myself from the limiting notions that work had to look a certain way, it became clear that the power I sought had nothing to do with position or fortune. It also became clear to me that all of my experiences were necessary for my personal growth. My travels brought me here to this place and gave me the tools I needed to be ready and able to fulfill my life's work.

By living my life in alignment with who I truly am, I am free to be all that I can be. Suddenly, the sky is the limit on how wonderful life can be. No longer must I struggle or strive to fit myself into a box that someone else has designed. I can live free to choose my own course and do what makes me happy.

I realized that I had been stumbling through life. It's not like you receive a book explaining how to live when you turn eighteen years old. There's no Life 101 taught in college. I wanted to have more control over how I chose to live. I was looking for the answers outside myself because I didn't have the answers...or so I thought.

But the answers are all there, just under the surface. Sometimes we're just not asking the right questions or we may not be ready for the answers. But when we are ready, the answers find us or we find the right coach or guide who helps us uncover what's been there all along. It all starts with becoming ready, willing, and open to explore the possibilities. You must be willing to dig deeper within yourself. The answers are revealed when you are ready to receive the answers.

When you start to look inside yourself, to discover the person that is you and to get to know who you are, that's when the clarity comes. With clarity, comes power and confidence. You move forward in life with self-assurance, you believe in this person called YOU. And, it all seems so simple, you'll wonder what the struggle was all about!

On my journey, I started to feel very powerful. All those years I asked the question, "How am I powerful?" wanting someone to show me the way. I never had a mentor, coach, or guide, and it took me years of personal struggle to find answers to that question. Had I known coaching existed, I certainly would have hired one and eliminated the struggle!

If the personal power each of us has to create whatever brings us the most joy is about self-mastery, what we really need is a guide to show us how to use our power to discover ourselves and to create an environment—a life—that supports us to open our buds and blossom, so we can become all that is possible for us to become. And this is what a good coach or the use of coaching skills by others does for you.

Self-discovery is about learning to come to know yourself newly. Look at yourself as your best friend, your most trusted advisor, the most important person in your life, and you'll see that the way you get to know others is by truly knowing yourself. In fact, you cannot truly know another person until you know yourself.

The secret to life is to live happily. It's that simple. How to do that, well, that's the question everyone asks. But the answer to that is simple as well. We just learn to make things more complicated than they need to be. Life really can be simple, effortless, and fun. Happiness looks different for everyone. You have to find your own way. There are some tools, however, that you can use to get you there. You need to access your personal power and make decisions that honor the person called you and that move you toward what feels good to you, using your integrity and your intuition as your guides. And you need to give yourself permission to feel good, giving up your relationship with struggle.

Thank you for joining me in this brief interlude. I trust that by sharing a piece of my journey you will better understand how a life focused on self-discovery and self-mastery will give you the confidence to move forward with style and grace.

In the next chapter, we discuss time and our relation with time. Our lives are made up of thousands of moments of time. Each moment is equally precious. How you choose to spend those moments makes a huge difference in the quality of your life.

Chapter Six

The Time of Your Life

"You'll seldom experience regret for anything that you've done. It is what you haven't done that will torment you. The message, therefore, is clear. Do it! Develop an appreciation for the present moment. Seize every second of your life and savor it. Value your present moments. Using them up in any self-defeating way means you've lost them forever."

—Dr. Wayne Dyer, psychologist and author

Time is a funny thing. When we're young, we want it to go faster— we want to be adults and to be responsible. As adults, we start learning how to be responsible and still fit fun into our lives. Between the kids and work, where will we find the time? Then we get older and we start to realize that life has a way of passing all too quickly. Could time slow down just a bit?

Who was it that said, "Time waits for no man"? I'm certain they were referring to women as well!

As people age, often they learn the lesson of time and they take less nonsense. They learn to stand up for themselves and to speak out for what they want. They learn that life is not to be feared, and a life not lived is worse than death. They learn that one cannot live in the past and that the future is not guaranteed.

Why wait until you get older to learn the lesson of urgency and the brevity of time? Why waste one moment living without purpose, doing

103

things you don't want to do, that are not in alignment with who you are, or that do not honor you?

Life equals time. Life is made up of thousands of moments of time. No one knows how much time you have. The quality of your life is directly proportional to how you choose to spend your time. You can invest in yourself—or not. You can enjoy your time—or not. You can live with regrets or choose forgiveness and make the most of every moment. You have a choice. The responsibility for the quality of your life—your time—is yours alone.

What a waste it would be for you to squander your time, frittering away hours, days, years on mindless, useless tasks. When you spend time doing things that do not bring you joy, or spend too much time doing things you hate or where you have no skill or talent, you waste your time—your life. Not only does your time slip away, but your life is unhappy and unfulfilled.

By learning to identify your gifts and strengths, developing them, and then designing your life so most of your time is spent using them, eliminating everything else that is not in alignment with supporting those gifts, you maximize your time and, in turn, your personal enjoyment and your rewards—both internal and external.

Time Enjoyment Model

"Time never stops to rest, never hesitates, never looks forward or backward. Life's raw material spends itself now, this moment—which is why how you spend your time is far more important than all the material possessions you may own or positions you may attain."

—Denis Waitley, American author

How much of your time is spent doing things you enjoy? People spend years living lives half full. They spend years in marriages that are "okay," in jobs that "pay the bills," in houses that "suit their needs," in the location that they've "always lived in." They've learned to sort of *put up with life* as it is because if they were to take a hard look at life, they would realize how unhappy they are, how unfulfilled they are.

This is the definition of a mediocre life.

Many people find it difficult to say what they want or to identify what makes them happy. Having no idea what you want can be an obstacle to living a great life. You learn to live by other people's rules or you settle for whatever opportunity comes to you never considering whether it's what you really want.

How do you know if something is what you want? You know by how it makes you *feel*. Feelings are very important for determining your level of happiness and enjoyment. They are your inner guidance system, your barometer. The more in tune you are with your feelings, the more you learn to experience your feelings, the richer your life will become.

As you explore yourself and discover the pieces of the puzzle of YOU, as you learn to eliminate the things that don't feel good from your life, you naturally move in the direction of what makes you feel good.

I've designed a model called the Time Enjoyment Model™, which I use with clients and in my lectures. It's composed of four quadrants representing your time and how you spend it. You identify whether you are skilled or not in comparison to whether you enjoy the activity or not. The purpose of the model is for you to increase your awareness of how much of your time is spent in each quadrant. As you go through your day, identify in which quadrant the activity belongs to help you to see how you spend your time. Time effectiveness is imperative for an enjoyable life. The more time you spend doing the things you love and are good at, the more enjoyable your life will be. Once you see how much time you spend in each quadrant, you can refocus your priorities and energies so you spend most of your time in Quadrant One, some time in Quadrant Two, and minimal amounts of time in Quadrants Three and Four.

Where do you spend most of your time? What percent of your time is spent in each quadrant? Use your journal to become more aware of how you treat your time as you answer the questions related to each quadrant.

Time Enjoyment Model

	Skilled	Under or Not Skilled
Enjoy	1	2
Do Not Enjoy	3	4

Quadrant One is where you find magic. This is where your passions live. This is where time melts away and you become one with all that is, where you find joy beyond your wildest dreams. This is where you belong.

Quadrant One is where your genius work resides. It includes all of the things that you love to do and you do well. Can you think of some things you do now that go in this square? This is where you want to spend most of your time. This is where you focus on mastery, excellence, achievement, and reap the most rewards, too. This is also where you maximize your talents, strengths, skills, and abilities to give all of yourself to the world. The more you focus your energies on spending all of your time—or most of it—in Quadrant One, the more fulfilled a life you will enjoy.

How much of your time is spent in this quadrant?

Quadrant Two represents those things where you are not skilled but you have fun doing them. Hobbies fit in here. Other things that you have fun doing but remain a novice will fall here. Can you list some activities that fall into this category?

Quadrant Two is where we spend most of our young adulthood. You're having a great time learning all kinds of things but you're not really skilled at anything. Eventually, you become skilled at something and it becomes a Quadrant One. Otherwise, it becomes a chore, something you're not skilled at and don't enjoy, and it moves to Quadrant Four. Even a hobby that you start spending more time doing, if you don't improve at it, you no longer find it as enjoyable.

You might also include here those things that you do that you find enjoyable but are not your genius work. These things are not the best use of your time—just be aware of how much time you're spending here. There's an opportunity cost; whenever you spend your time doing one thing, you (obviously) cannot be doing something else. Every time you make a choice to do one thing, you lose that time. You want to make smart choices about how you spend your time. Although Quadrant Two is a good place to be, there needs to be a level of caution as to how much time you spend here.

How much time do you spend in Quadrant Two?

Quadrant Three represents the time you spend performing those things where you exhibit skill, you can do it well, but you hate doing it. Maybe your job falls here. Maybe cooking or cleaning falls into this category. What are some activities you can identify that belong in this quadrant?

There are people who spend their lives in Quadrant Three, unhappy but perhaps not clear how to change their lives. After many years in the same position, you might find your work falls in Quadrant Three. The job is boring. It no longer challenges you or you have just lost your desire for it. It's also possible that you don't realize how good you are and haven't yet learned to value your abilities. Perhaps you underestimate yourself.

When you don't value yourself or your skills, you can become complacent. Your work might even become mediocre. When you don't see the value in your work, when you are not aware of how special you are, and you don't appreciate your work, you start to "go through the motions." You may find it difficult to accept compliments from others, or it's possible you're not given enough positive feedback or the reinforcement you need in order to learn how your work impacts others. Bosses can be stingy with praise and are often quick to criticize.

It also happens that when you learn something new, the information is incorporated into your current knowledge base. Then, you discount it. In other words, it's easy to say that since you know it, everyone must know it. You must resist the temptation to do this. Don't discount what you know! It leads you to undervalue your skills and abilities. People stay in jobs too long where their skills are not valued because they don't value the skills themselves!

A Walk Through the Clouds: Discounting Your Knowledge

"...the task is not so much to see what no one has yet seen, but to think what nobody yet has thought about that which everybody sees."
—Arthur Schopenhaur, German philosopher

Mark wanted to be a teacher. He had two more classes to go before completing his master's degree. But he needed to return to school to finish first. What held him back?

"What do I have to teach that they don't already know?" he said.

No one knows what you know. No one else has the same mix of background, experience, perspective, education, upbringing, and understanding as you do. There is no one else like you.

By thinking you have nothing to offer, you hold yourself back. You have *you* to share with the world. Don't keep your thoughts and ideas to yourself. Share them.

COACHING TIP: When you learn something new, it becomes integrated into what you already know. You think about it and somehow it all fits together; you make sense of it. Learning to use the knowledge you've obtained over your lifetime is the purpose for learning. Knowledge gained without challenge holds no power, just untapped potential. How sad. Whatever voice inside you that tells you that what you know doesn't matter, just tell it you didn't ask for its opinion! All of your experiences count and together they create something amazing. Only you know what it all means and as you share what you've learned, it solidifies your knowledge and understanding.

Knowledge is meant to be shared, and tested, and challenged. You have to learn how to use what you've learned in a way that makes you happy. There is no one with your style who can do it better than you. You are the best person for this job. Learn to express yourself and all you know in the way that makes you most happy.

If you value yourself and your skills, and you are not valued where you work, instead of pointing your finger, accept responsibility for where you are. Are you doing everything you can to get recognized or be promoted? If you are and they are not noticing, find another employer who will value you the way you deserve. Take an assessment of what you want in an employer and a boss; what's important to you in the way of recognition and appreciation?

Finding yourself in Quadrant Three can be a good eye-opener. Are you underestimating how well you do the job? Is it the skill you dislike or the environment? Do you enjoy anything about the skill? Perhaps it's not the skill that you dislike; perhaps it's how you have to use the skill.

Charlotte was the supervisor of a department and became a client when she was passed over for a promotion. She was angry and wanted to find another job.

Charlotte had many skills. One of the things she enjoyed was the theater. She volunteered directing plays at a local playhouse. She often dreamed of having her own theater one day.

The reality was that in her current position, she directed the staff much like the way she conducted the actors in her plays. She was the director on the job! The more she realized how well her skills and talents played out in this position, she realized how grateful she was that she didn't get the promotion. As the manager, she would have different responsibilities and her work would look different. Although her current job may not be where she wants to stay forever, she found a new appreciation for her position and was able to support the person who got the promotion without being angry over not being chosen. She was right where she needed to be.

What activities fall into Quadrant Three for you?

Quadrant Four relates to the time you spend doing things you don't enjoy and you're not very good at. The time spent here will be your least fulfilling. In fact, it's usually pretty energy draining.

Spending time in Quadrant Four means that you are settling for less than excellence. You cannot experience excellence in Quadrant Four, since you are not skilled here. Whatever activities you are doing that don't bring you joy, eliminate them. Just stop doing them. If they absolutely must get done, then hire someone else to do it—someone for whom this activity is a number one!

That is a really important point: If there is something that for you is a Four, then look for someone who finds it a One.

When you do any type of task or project, ask yourself whether you are the best person for the job. How do you feel about doing this task? If it doesn't feel good to work on it, then it probably belongs in Quadrant Three or Four. Something that's a Three or Four for you is a One or a Two for someone else. You may think that doing it yourself is easier: "I know I hate doing this, but I do it better than anyone else. It's easier if I just get it done." It may be easier in the moment but since this is not your genius work, spending time here steals time away from focusing on what you do best. Just because you *can* do something doesn't mean you *should*. Whatever the task, however, it is someone else's genius work or it could be theirs in the making. When you consider this perspective, you start looking for ways to give away your Threes and Fours! Not only will it reduce your stress and your workload, you'll be bringing out the best of those around you by allowing them to do what they love to do.

Imagine your life spent entirely in Quadrant One. Imagine how wonderful it will feel to only be doing those things that are most enjoyable for you and in which you excel! It's a glorious feeling to spend all of your time with the people, in the places, and doing the things you love the most. And if you're not, then what's that about?

You choose how you spend your time. You decide the best way to live your life. If you are spending time doing things that do not enrich your life, that do not develop you personally or professionally, or that do not bring you joy, then you are losing time—time that you cannot retrieve.

Time is more precious than gold. It cannot be bought or saved. And although many people try, you cannot rush through time to get more of it; you just lose it faster. Treat it with care. Learn to use it wisely.

EXERCISE: Living the Life of Your Dreams

Imagine living in Quadrant One all of the time. You've created the space in your life to do only those things you love doing and that are the best use of your talents and skills. Imagine the peace, the serenity, the joy. It's awesome living here.

Imagine getting up in the morning so excited that you're alive and that you've been given another opportunity to do the very things you love. Imagine getting dressed in your favorite, most comfortable clothes and getting in your car, which you absolutely love. You drive to work and the ride is joyful. You pull up to the building where you work and you are so glad to be there, to have the opportunity to use your strengths and skills to make a difference in the world.

People are glad to see you. They enjoy you and you enjoy them. They challenge you to be your best and you get to contribute to their growth as well. At the end of the day, you feel refreshed yet ready to leave to do some of your other favorite things. Maybe you enjoy cooking so you stop at the store and pick up some ingredients for dinner. Or perhaps you don't like to cook and your spouse has dinner waiting for you. Or you meet a friend at a favorite restaurant. All your time is spent doing exactly what makes you happy.

At the end of the evening, you have a bedtime routine that is refreshing and relaxing. You are ready to end this wonderful day to start again tomorrow.

This is how incredible life can be.

What keeps us from living in Quadrant One? Why aren't all of us living there all the time?

Many things get in the way of our path to living this way. One is awareness, or the lack of it. Simply not knowing that this is what life can be will cause people not to pursue it. Also, not knowing how to achieve this kind of life keeps people stuck where they are.

Moving your life into Quadrant One is a journey. There are lessons to learn along the way and growing to do. The *journey* is your life, so enjoy the journey. The journey of becoming aware of who you are and the process of moving your life into Quadrant One is very exciting, enjoyable, and gratifying. Each step of the way is an accomplishment to be acknowledged and celebrated. The journey is what's important because the journey—how you live each day—is your life.

With each day, you become more aware of yourself and how you feel about the things you do and the things that the world presents you. And as you learn to honor yourself and make decisions that are in your best interest, you move quietly and assuredly into Quadrant One and the life you love to be living.

Clearing Your Path

In order to pave the way for you to create a fabulous life, you have to eliminate those things that do not bring you joy. What *don't* you want to be doing? By becoming aware of the things that drain your energy and deplete you, you can start to eliminate them, creating space for the things that add to your life.

Identify those things you do that fall into Quadrants Three and Four. By identifying things here, you can create a plan of action to pass them on to someone else or give them up entirely. You want to create a deliberate plan of action in order to honor yourself.

What are the things that you can delegate, eliminate, or outsource? What are the things in your life that you do simply because they keep you busy? As you move forward on your journey, you must become open and aware to what you are doing and the true intention behind your actions. If you are keeping busy, could it be that you are hiding from something? One client used to stay very late at work because she didn't want to be at home; it was more pleasant to be at work. Another client stayed at work late because she didn't have the skills to delegate effectively. Another client structured her life where she worked weekends and nights to avoid being with her husband. Is there something you're doing to avoid being with someone or to avoid facing something? Give yourself permission to get honest, deal with it, and remove it from your life completely. You'll create space for what you want, you'll have a lot more energy, and you'll eliminate a lot of unnecessary stress. What are you holding onto?

Whatever it is, awareness of it will help you to honor yourself. Making the tough decisions helps move it out of your subconscious where it's habit and it's draining your life force and into the open where you can face it. It's never preferable to live a lie rather than face the truth. To have your life *look good* but not *feel good* is not living; it's existing. That's not success and in your heart, you know it. To not honor yourself, to choose not to do what you know is right for you, is a crime against yourself.

Busy doesn't always mean hiding. Sometimes it just means having too much on your plate, not knowing how to say "no" or delegate, having too many responsibilities, being scattered and lacking focus and direction, or simply believing that this is how you're supposed to live.

A Walk Through the Clouds: The Busyness Trap

"I'm just so busy." These words are the excuse for why we don't exercise, why we don't call, why we don't accomplish more of the things that bring us joy. It's an excuse.

Why *are* you so busy? If you're not happy, not doing the things that bring you joy, and don't have the time and energy to live the way you want, what are you doing with your time? It will never get better until you decide to do things differently.

We've all heard the phrase, "If you want something done, give it to a busy person." My father used to say that all the time and I thought it was a good thing to be a busy person. It meant that you were dependable, you got things done. That's a good thing.

Not if you're the busy person.

Busy people wind up being the dumping ground. They're the ones everyone gives their work to. The busy person sets unrealistic expectations for how much they can accomplish in a certain time frame. They also have difficulty saying "no." I had to learn this lesson myself. I kept pushing myself to do it all and others learned that they could keep giving me things to do because they knew I'd get it done.

I finally realized how I was hurting. I was always busy while others had time for conversations, coffee, and lunch breaks. I was not given respect; in fact, it seemed the more I pushed myself, the less respect I received. I was not reaping the rewards of my efforts. People were using me. And I felt abused.

I also realized that I had the power to change my reality. If I wanted things to be different, I had to change the way I was being. Others can certainly ask me to do things; I cannot control what they do. I needed to learn to care for myself and to say "yes" to only those things that were the best use of my time and for what I was being paid to do. I needed to value my time so I could teach others to value it too. When you keep doing more and more, people assume you can handle it. They don't know what's on your plate. When you start to set limits, you change people's expectations of you. You start to own both your work and your time.

COACHING TIP: "Busy" often results in feeling overwhelmed, which usually means it's time to simplify. Do less. Schedule less on your calendar. Take on fewer assignments and projects. Reconnect with yourself by taking more time to just be. Gently shift your lifestyle so you have more "being" time.

Start saying "no" to all of the things you don't want to do. Find someone else to do them—either delegate or hire someone.

Stop doing other people's work and stop taking responsibility for other people's work. Learn how to redirect people. If you learn to say "no," they'll find someone else or learn to do it themselves. If you feel uncomfortable saying "no," perhaps to your boss, then say something like: "I would be happy to do that for you. And I have X, Y, and Z that I am working on. Which project would you prefer I work on today?" By letting your boss know what you are working on and allowing him or her to set your priorities, you take responsibility for your time, honoring yourself as well as his or her requests. The control you have is over you and your inner state of being. When you give up the frantic pace and set limits on your time, while there's still hustle and chaos around you, you remain calm and at peace.

As you start to slow down, you'll find that you have plenty of time to do everything you want to do—just not all in the same moment! There is more than enough time to accomplish what you want over the course of your lifetime. This is a shift from living in scarcity and lack to an abundance mentality. "Busy" distracts you from looking up at the horizon and where you are headed. Learn to slow down and you'll be able to enjoy life, rather than just "get it done."

"Busy" is a societal game. If you stay busy, you don't have time to think, you don't have time to question, and you don't have time to feel. You certainly don't have time to recognize your inner voice.

When you tell others, "I'm so busy," it doesn't feel good on the receiving end either. If you are continually busy when people call, they stop calling. It's as if you're telling them that you don't have time for them. The message you're giving is that "things" are more important than "people." Always, always, put people before things. Stop what you are doing when someone else is speaking and give them your attention. This saves time because you are present for them and are able to hear what they say, resulting in fewer miscommunications. It requires your time and attention to put people first, but the rewards are invaluable.

Recognize that you can change the rules. For example, is there an unwritten rule that says you must answer the phone? If you are busy and focused on completing something, then it's up to you to eliminate distractions, including answering the phone or email.

Maintaining a state of perpetual busyness is not healthy. In fact, it is stressful and this lifestyle has physical ramifications. When you allow yourself to slow down, you offer yourself the opportunity to enjoy the present.

A Walk Through the Clouds: The Adrenaline Lifestyle

Busy can also be a symptom of an adrenaline lifestyle. The use of adrenaline as a drug is prevalent in our society today. After all, you need energy to survive. You eat and exercise to give your body energy, alternating with periods of rest and renewal for maximizing your body's resources and faculties. Getting enough rest and sleep is an important but often neglected part of enjoying your life journey. There are many different ways to get energy; some are healthier than others. Passion, pleasure, and joy all add energy to your life force. These are positive energy sources. Negative energy sources include sugar, caffeine, unmet needs, anger, winning, drama, and conflict. These will give you energy too, but at a cost.

Adrenaline (also called epinephrine) is a natural steroid produced by the adrenal glands in response to the perception of harm. You know it as the "fight-or-flight" mechanism. Many people, however, use it daily to give them the energy they need to get through the day. As a steroid, adrenaline helps improve concentration so you think clearly; it also provides you with tremendous strength, agility, and speed for you to act swiftly. It fools you into believing this is an efficient way to live so it becomes your energy of choice, you find ways to produce it on demand, and it becomes a way of life.

Although it sounds wonderful, it takes a lot of energy from the body's systems to maintain this heightened state, so at the end of the day, you crash. Used daily, eventually it harms the tissues of the body and can result in heart attacks, insomnia, depression, anxiety, strokes, and other stress-related illnesses. Your body responds to stress with the release of adrenaline, and it is this substance that causes you harm over time. It is the release of this substance on a regular basis that doctors want you to avoid when they tell you to decrease stress in your life.

As an adrenaline junkie, you display certain characteristics including being rushed, always busy, often late, known for getting it done, and juggling multiple projects; you might talk fast and become easily annoyed or frustrated.

If you are constantly living in this hyped-up mode, you may be feeling as though life is just passing you by, like you are not an active participant. Spiraling downward and out of control, you feel like something has to give.

You can stop it and take back your control over your life. Identify the areas or things you do to trigger the release of adrenaline. Are you driving too fast, participating in too many projects, or taking responsibility for other people? What other things can you identify that drain you of energy and concentration?

- Do you worry about what others think of you?
- Are you deadline-driven?
- Are you in emotional or physical pain?
- Do you set goals based on your own standards or on others' expectations?
- Do you have any unresolved issues that distract you from being fully present?
- Are you a procrastinator or a perfectionist?
- Do you often run late?
- Are you the type of person that thrives on a chaotic environment, creating crises such as financial messes or relationship problems just to get hyped up?

If any of these situations sound familiar, then you may be using adrenaline to get you "up." Accustomed to creating stress and thinking of everything as a stressor, you have created a life where control is at the mercy of the circumstances of the day. It's not what happens to you, but rather your response to what happens that causes stress. If you are a worrier, if you lack trust, if you are not grounded in your sense of self, you may respond with a shot of adrenaline. Respond this way often enough and it becomes a habit; it becomes a way of life.

There are healthier ways to live.

This kind of exploration allows you to open the door to understanding *how you are being* in the world. Take a deep breath. Imagine what life would be like if you were at peace, relaxed, and calm. You are free; you get to know yourself better; you're more aware and in touch because you're not rushing through life; your relationships improve; you have more energy for the things you enjoy; and there's a sense of trust—trust in yourself and faith that things will all work out exactly the way they are supposed to. There's no need for you to push, stress, or rush. You live your life in a different, more deliberate pace.

I have to admit, I was once a typical adrenaline junkie, in a constant state of "rush," always just on time or a few minutes late, deadline-driven, and the get-it-done queen, which also meant "dumping ground." When I first heard this term "adrenaline junkie," I identified with it immediately. I didn't enjoy being this way, and I certainly didn't like feeling as though I was out of control.

It takes time—years even—to change the kind of person you are being into someone who is peaceful, not reactionary, and calm regardless of what is going on around you. This is a journey toward grace.

You must learn to slow down. Identify those things that trigger the adrenaline release for you so you can stop it. Learn to simplify your life. At some point, you'll slow down so much that you get bored; you don't know quite what to do with yourself. Eventually, you figure it out and start to add things that make you feel good and look for healthier energy sources without the negative side effects.

Music, a good book, good friends, laughter, meditation, love, nature, and exercise or yoga are all things that add to your life force. Try some on for size and you'll see that life will take on new meaning. It won't be about rushing through life but rather enjoying the time you have here.

COACHING TIP: Once you learn to live without adrenaline and you develop a new state of awareness, you can feel it in your body when the adrenaline kicks in. Something happens, perhaps it's one too many projects or a new deadline, and you start to become panicky. You can actually feel the adrenaline rushing through your veins. You feel the anxiety start to build. The enzyme that breaks down adrenaline isn't contained in the bloodstream, so it needs to be produced and then released, which takes time, so the adrenaline stays in your system for a while.

When this happens, stop what you are doing and rest. Take some deep breaths. Eventually, it will pass. If you are conscious to it, you can choose peace. Deliberately choose a slower pace and trust that it will all be accomplished. Without the rush and panic, you can consider other options to the tasks you face. What are the true priorities? Does it all need to get done immediately or can something wait until the next day? Gather support of others. Who is the best person for the job? Who can you ask for help? What can you eliminate? When you stay calm and enter a state of trust, you know that it will all work out fine. Things always do.

Every situation presents you with an opportunity to learn a lesson in order to move you forward and beyond this type of happening. This reduces the possibility of this type of occurrence happening again in the future, enabling you to make the most of your time. Whenever you experience anything there are two levels of experience going on: one, to get through the situation, and two, to look beyond the immediate situation in order to create a system where this never happens again. This ensures you learn the lesson so you can move on to learn other life lessons. You must be open to this kind of learning, however, and look for the lesson.

Where are you operating in crisis mode? Start shifting to a more proactive operating system. Do you need to start delegating more? Do you need to learn how to ask for help? Whatever it is, look for what you need to change so you eliminate the possibility of this same type of situation occurring again creating negative patterns in your life.

Invest Your Time

Every moment offers you the opportunity to invest your time or waste your time. Is what you are doing at any given moment the best way to spend your time? How much time are you wasting?

Ultimately, you want to eliminate the things that do not add value to you and invest your time in things, conversations, projects that honor you and add value to your life. There are numerous "time wasters." Some of them include the following:

- Procrastinating
- Perfectionism
- Arguing—not listening
- Taking things personally
- Interruptions/distractions
- Not delegating
- Not prioritizing
- Unclear goals/objectives
- No plan—busy in action
- Disorganized
- Lack of knowledge
- Afraid to ask for assistance
- Settling for less than excellence
- Not enforcing personal boundaries

- Unable to say no to things/people/projects
- Comparing self to others
- Concerns over what other people think
- Unresolved issues, living in the past
- Worry about the future, living in "what ifs"
- Gossip, negative conversations
- Too much TV, computer games, and so on
- Unfinished projects

Do any of these ring true for you? Are there others that aren't listed that waste your time? Many of these are obstacles that have been identified in this book and all of them can be overcome. Things that waste your time will drain your energy and also interfere with your achieving higher levels of happiness and fulfillment. Awareness is critical so you can create a vision for success and start to design what you want.

COACHING NOTE: Understanding Procrastination

"My mother always told me I wouldn't amount to anything because I procrastinate. I said, 'Just wait.'"
—Judy Tenuta, comedian

Procrastination isn't necessarily a bad thing, depending on why you are procrastinating. Sometimes you procrastinate because you don't want to do something, but you have to. Create urgency and do it or delegate it if you can. If it's an item in Quadrant Three or Four, then find a way to have someone else take over the task. Teach them if you must. This is something you want off your plate; either schedule it and get it done, or give it away.

Sometimes you procrastinate because you don't want to do something and it doesn't need to get done. Well, instead of putting it off, eliminate it. Don't do it. By thinking about it, even though it's not something you need to do, it's draining your energy and wasting your time.

Sometimes you don't do something because you don't know how. Learn or give it to someone else to do. Part of accepting responsibility for yourself is changing the way you get things done to a more effective way, a way that serves you.

Sometimes you procrastinate because it isn't your responsibility but somehow you believe it is. (Are you a martyr?) Give it back to the person responsible and stop taking on projects that are not the best use of your time and talents. This serves no one.

Rarely do you procrastinate because you are lazy. Usually, it's because you took on too much, it's stuff you don't want to do, or you don't have systems in place to get it all done. Sometimes you don't have the energy because you're spending too much time and wasting energy in Quadrants Three and Four. Sometimes you put stuff off because you're not skilled at making decisions. Clutter is simply delayed decision-making and often builds when you don't have systems in place and/or are too attached to your stuff. It's important that you learn what procrastinating looks like for you so you can clear it up.

If you need to eliminate clutter, then commit to doing it. Set up a regular time each week for a few hours; get a friend to help, and clear it all away—a little at a time. Simplify your environment. Separate what you need to have from the nice-to-haves. Create systems to keep you organized such as coming in with the mail and standing by the trash while you open and sort it. Then, deal with it immediately; put the bills wherever you sit to pay your bills and throw out whatever you won't read; put the magazines where they go. Organizing is not something you do once and are done with it. Each day there are new things to integrate into your life. The more you learn, the easier it gets. Take a course on organizing or hire a coach who specializes in organizing. I recommend Kerul Kassel at www.NewLeafSystems.com, an expert in organizing and eliminating procrastination. Or visit www.FlyLady.com. Do whatever it takes to resolve the issue. Until you do, you waste precious time thinking about all you have to do instead of enjoying everything you have.

Start becoming more careful about the things that you say "yes" to. Choose how you spend your time in a way that best serves you. Take each commitment you make very seriously. How you fulfill your commitments says a lot about who you are and where you are on your personal development continuum. As you become more aware of how you use your time, and you eliminate things that are not in your best interest, learn to protect your time and take your time seriously so you only take on things that bring you joy.

A Walk Through the Clouds: Perfectionism

"Aim for success, not perfection. Never give up your right to be wrong, because then you will lose the ability to learn new things and move forward with your life. Remember that fear always lurks behind perfectionism. Confronting your fears and allowing yourself the right to be human can, paradoxically, make yourself a happier and more productive person."

—Dr. David M. Burns, author of *The Feeling Good Handbook*

How does perfectionism serve you? Striving for perfect is often tied closely with self-esteem resulting in not finishing things, not starting things for fear that your results will not be "perfect," or having a stressful experience living in fear or making a mistake.

Mistakes aren't bad; in fact, they're necessary for your growth. Mistakes offer you the opportunity to learn something new or to do something better. They are perfect.

Mistakes don't communicate anything about *who you are*; they are about "what" you've done. You didn't know enough, you were hasty, or things didn't happen the way you anticipated. How you handle your mistakes communicates volumes about who you are and where you are on your personal development continuum. And this is all that matters—not that you make mistakes but that you learn and grow from the experience.

Perfectionists often believe that no one else can do a better job and that they must do it all by themselves, the result of which is that you keep working to get things done and you're stressed while everyone else seems to be having fun. You're at work and they're playing golf or going shopping.

By learning to delegate to others who are more skilled in those areas that you are not, by learning to give back the work to people that should be doing what's been dumped on you, you create space in your time. This frees you to do more of the things that are your genius work and where you have the most fun. It also allows others to do their genius work.

I am a reformed perfectionist myself. It was 1993 and I got seven wrong on my microbiology final, which was a 100-multiple-choice-question exam, and I was angry. I was disappointed. How could I get seven wrong? After beating myself up for a while, I realized how silly I was being. After all, I still got an "A." But I wasn't perfect. I finally realized that what was most important was that I learned the material and I did my best. And by focusing on that, it was perfect. When you shift to seeking excellence instead of perfectionism, you allow yourself headroom to maneuver. And there will always be greater and greater heights to reach for because excellence knows no bounds.

COACHING TIP: If you are striving for unrealistic expectations, you will always be disappointed. Look for what is already perfect and strive for excellence instead. When you focus on excellence, it takes the stress off of you to perform and lets you just be your best. When you focus on excellence, you also create the space for others to be their best and for it to be okay to make mistakes. Use mistakes as opportunities to learn and to grow. They bring your attention to things you didn't know you needed to know. That's the way life is…and it's perfect.

By becoming more aware of how you spend your time, you can identify those areas that require your attention and make better choices.

Pay attention to how you feel about the conversations you have and the things you do. Is what you're doing contributing to your personal or professional development? Is it uplifting? Is it making you a better person? Are you learning something? Or is what you are doing draining your energy?

Is it something that you yourself must do or should it be delegated? Are you the best person for the job? Is this the best way to spend your time right now?

Do you feel comfortable in this conversation? Are you "dancing" in conversation where there's an interesting exchange? Or is it a struggle to express yourself?

If what you are doing is not adding to your development or is not enjoyable, then it is depleting you.

Learning to invest your time means spending your time in ways that bring out your best and stretch you to become more. Learning to develop yourself personally and professionally, dealing with your past, working on self-discovery and self-improvement as well as educating yourself both formally and through reading books and staying current in your field, all add value to you, expand your thinking, and add to your capacity to do more and to be more.

The value of your time is what you have to offer an employer. It is your only commodity. The more you educate your mind, the more you practice your trade or skill, the better you become at managing your emotions, the quicker you become at solving problems or accomplishing tasks. With more education and critical thinking ability, you can command more money. Money is merely an exchange of value. You are paid money (and benefits) for the quality or the value of your time.

Take your time seriously. Come to accept urgency to life—to living the way that brings you joy—and you'll come to this place where each moment matters. It doesn't mean that you must fill your time with useless stuff to do, rather learn to balance doing with allowing the universe to do. This means you want to be purposeful in the things you do so you have time to simply be, allow, and enjoy.

Setting Bold Limits

What other things get in the way of your life enjoyment? People? Your environment? If time is your life, you must learn to become very protective of your time. If it doesn't bring you joy, why do it? If it isn't fun and you're not learning anything, what's the point?

This is true even in business. My client, Jane, said that their department has conference call "clinics" each month where everyone comes to listen to a speaker who she found to be quite boring. Last time, one person was reading a book and others were having conversations. What's the point of this clinic if no one is paying attention? I didn't understand. What a waste of company time and resources! If there is no benefit, then there is a cost.

In this example, here you have ten or more people not doing what they need to be doing and getting paid to do something that is not adding to them in any way. Either make the meeting beneficial so it adds value or only have the people attend who need whatever is being reviewed in that session. It's about taking your employees' time more seriously.

People don't always know what the best way to spend their time is. If you are in a leadership position, you may need to teach them. You teach them by how you treat their time as well as your own time.

Taking your time more seriously means learning to say "no" and setting clear boundaries for others and high standards for yourself. Without boundaries, you become a dumping ground. You become resentful. Resentfulness is really about you not addressing something in your life. Accepting responsibility for the results you achieve in your life means learning to recognize when you are allowing the poor habits or unmet needs of others to spill into your space. By learning to speak up for yourself, you send a clear message to others about how you respect yourself and your time. You teach others how you want to be treated by how you treat yourself.

Taking your time seriously means choosing your commitments with care. When someone presents an opportunity for you, resist the temptation to just say "yes." Take a moment—or as much time as you need—to consider the consequences or impact of taking on this commitment. Is this the best use of your time and talents? Will this move you closer to your vision of success? Do you have the "space in time" to give this commitment or project the attention it requires? In other words, will you be able to fit this into your schedule without difficulty or stress? Will you be able to follow through? And most importantly, do you want to take this on at this time in your life?

The reality is that just because you have the skills and the time, if it's not where you want to put your energies right now, then you need to say "no." When you are intentional about your commitments, you'll find that you do less and the commitments you choose are those things you want to be doing, which makes life effortless and fun. And you'll find it easier to manage your schedule and see things through to completion.

In the Scheme of Things

When you consider the millions of years the earth has existed, your years here on this planet are merely a speck of time. It's easy to get caught in the minutiae of the day: the problems that seem insurmountable, the baby who won't be consoled, the traffic that won't move, the dry cleaning that got lost, or the project that won't be ready for another week. In those moments of frustration, if you take a wider view of life, you see how unimportant and insignificant those things are.

When you get stuck in the minutiae, you fail to recognize what this action or task means in the bigger picture of your life. If you take a wider view and look at your lifespan, how important is what you're doing at this moment? How important is what you're choosing to focus on?

Each moment, in and of itself, is unimportant and yet, paradoxically, each moment is very important to move you closer to that point of success you seek. If you know what success looks like, then you need to keep that vision in sight. And as you work in the moment, ask yourself whether this thing you are doing is moving you in the direction you want to go.

When you are lost in the small details, it feels as though every little thing is large and powerful; the molehills are mountains, so to speak. It's as if you are standing in the forest trying to find your way through. Looking up at the trees, they appear so massive. You awe at the wonder of them. But as you search through the forest for your path, they can get in your way; you can't see through them. All you see is one massive tree after another. It can become overwhelming.

When you look at your life from a higher view, it's as if you are flying above the forest to see the entire landscape. You can appreciate the trees from this view too, but no longer do they appear to be obstacles in the way, rather you can see the patterns of their placement in the forest and how you had to go around here in order to find the path that darted out from over there. You look at the years and the decades, you can see over time how your life is progressing and how certain events impacted the direction of your life. From this different perspective, you can see how life events moved you in certain directions and that the awareness, teachings, or understandings came to you only after you walked a certain path or experienced certain events. You cannot get that perspective when you are in the forest or in the day-to-day of life. You have to take a wider view.

As you learn to see things from this new perspective, you keep in touch with what matters most in your life. Taking a wider view of life means you keep your eye on the horizon as well as deal with the tasks of the day. You have to look up every so often to be sure you are still traveling in the direction you want to go. Make sure that what's most important to you remains a constant focus of your time and attention.

It also helps you to plan your life. Each decade provides you with lessons. Your life, from decade to decade, takes on a different focus. In your twenties, the focus of your attention is different than it will be in your forties. When you keep your eye on the horizon, you're not just living for the day; you are also keeping an eye on what's coming. That way, as you chart your course for your life, you won't be surprised by life. You can plan for your kids to go to college. You can plan for your own retirement. There is this connection with how you live today and the creation of a fabulous future.

In the next chapter, you will learn different ways to honor yourself. It is the day-to-day moments that do make a difference and add up over time as you make choices that honor you, that bring you closer to living in harmony with your true self.

Coaching Challenge

- Examine how you spend your time and identify things that fall in each of the four quadrants of the Time Enjoyment Model©. Start identifying things in Quadrants Three and Four that you can eliminate or that you need to delegate and focus your attention on doing more of the things that fall in Quadrant One.

- What do you need to simplify in your life? Is there an area where you feel overwhelmed? Make a commitment to do less. Clear your evening schedule. Eliminate or limit your volunteer projects to create space in your schedule for the time being. Identify those things that can be eliminated from your schedule. Slow down so you can experience yourself in the moment. If you are rushing through life, what is it that you hope to achieve? Happiness and personal fulfillment happen in the moments of the day.

- Where are you procrastinating? Whatever is on your plate, schedule it on your calendar and get it done. You'll feel so relieved when you're all caught up. Create a system to stay that way and to get things done as soon as they come to your attention. Become the kind of person who takes on fewer commitments so you can take them seriously and follow through every time.

- Take a view of your life from above the forest. Write in your journal about the last decade of your life. What has been the major focus? Make a list of the experiences you had— such as completed your degree, changed jobs twice, got married, had one child, experienced bad illness, experienced death of one friend, and so on. What do you want the next decade of your life to be focused on? Some examples might be: personal development so you feel more grounded in being you, finances and making more money, raising your children and being present for them. It doesn't need to be specific behaviors of what you'll do; just an overall guide for what you want to focus on. Then, each year, instead of New Year's resolutions, you can set goals that you want to achieve. Evaluate your progress at the end of each year and then set new goals to take you further along your path to where you ultimately want to go. By identifying this now, you can focus on making it happen.

Chapter Seven

The New Rules: Honor Yourself

"You yourself, as much as anybody in the entire universe deserve your love and affection."
—Buddha

As you learn more about yourself, you realize how amazing you are: the way you think, the way your body works, the special things there are to know about you. Life is the gift given to you for your enjoyment. You cannot enjoy anyone else's life; you can only enjoy yours.

You think, you feel, you bleed, you endure, you win, you stumble, you succeed. You can experience emotions by watching others. You can appreciate the triumphs and defeats of others. You can feel empathy and compassion for others. But without paying due attention to your own life, you will miss the best of what life has to offer.

Many people live vicariously through the lives of others. Watching the soaps or the reality television shows makes people feel as though they have an exciting life. But it's not real. It's someone else's life. It's not your reality. It's someone acting out a reality while you sit on the sidelines and watch.

Life is so much bigger than that.

No one can tell you how to live your life. You can read books about what others have done; some books give you advice, but only you can decide what path to take; only you can decide which suggestions to use in order to create a great life for yourself. You can read the story about another's journey but it's almost as though their path closes behind

128

them. What makes one person successful and fulfilled cannot bring another the same level of satisfaction. We are all different. You must chart your own course, discover your own path to success and happiness, and go for it.

Your answers for living a great life are found by doing what makes you feel good and no one knows what makes you feel good or what brings out the best in you but you. Learning how to do *that*, well, that's why you're reading this book!

The prescription for creating and living a great life is getting to know yourself, accepting yourself for who you are, and honoring and loving yourself. By focusing your time and energy on opening up your heart, mind, and soul to understand how you think and behave, what you are all about, what makes you tick, what makes you happy, and then making choices that honor you in all your splendid glory, you experience the best of what life is all about and you create a life that supports and nourishes the best in you.

Putting Yourself First

You are the most important person in your life. Do you live your life as if that were true? The fact is that without you, you have nothing.

Many people are taught that others are more important. The message is that your children or your spouse come first, that their happiness is more important than your own. Women, especially, have tremendous difficulty conceiving of taking care of their own needs first. Caretakers—both men and women—are known to place the needs of others before their own so much so that often they get lost in their caretaking. They learn to hide. Caretaking becomes their life. It's a safe place to be because if you focus your entire life on the needs of others then you don't have to worry about or plan your own life. You don't have to explore the possibilities that exist for you because your life is spent taking care of others under the notion that this is good. This is noble. This is what you are meant to do. And so long as you are happy and complete with your life choice, this is fine. You don't, however, want to reach the end of your life wishing you had done more for yourself or had done something else. The fact is that there will always be someone needing help, someone needing more—it will never be enough. You need to set limits. You need to determine what to give and how much to give without sacrificing yourself or your happiness in the process.

When you give too much of yourself, you start to feel resentment. Resentment is a kind of anger; it's not anger at another for what they have done. Rather you're angry at yourself for allowing it or for not doing anything to stop or correct it. Resentment is really anger at self.

If you don't take care of yourself, you will wind up needing the very charity that you so graciously give others. You have a responsibility to take care of yourself in every possible way. If you do not plan for your retirement because you don't plan ahead, if you constantly give money to your children or family, or if you live beyond your means, who will care for you when you can no longer work?

You are responsible to care for your health. If you get sick, go to the doctor. Don't feel guilty for calling into work when you are sick. What's that about? Ask yourself what your body is telling you. Illness is one way the body communicates to us. When we don't listen to our intuition, our inner knowing, then it turns to our body to force us to listen. When you don't feel well, you are unable to give to anyone *but* yourself.

When you are accustomed to putting the needs of others above your own and when you look to others to give you self-confidence and assurance, then taking a sick day seems wrong even when it's the right thing to do. Worrying about what others think of you and focusing on pleasing others are ineffective ways to make decisions in your best interest.

COACHING NOTE: Permission

Do you need permission to make yourself a priority?

You have it. You have permission to do whatever is right for you. You have permission to free yourself from any bondage—self-imposed or other—so you can enjoy every part of your life.

Although I can say that to you, it is you who must give permission to yourself. The fact is that you are here, on this earth at this time, to discover and maximize your gifts. To do anything less is not honoring yourself.

Give yourself permission to do what's right for you. Learn to take good care of your body, mind, and spirit. The thing to know is that this is a *journey* into self-care, not a destination. The destination *is* the journey. Each day offers you a new opportunity to learn more about yourself, to care more deeply about yourself, and to do something special to make you feel good.

What are some things that make you feel good? Take some time to list some of your favorite things to do.

Body

Massage	Touch—sex, hugs
Visit a spa	Exercise
Manicure and pedicure	Tai chi, yoga, martial arts
Body lotion	Sports
Bath	Dressing in comfortable clothes

Mind

Reading	Skills training, conferences
Education, lifelong learning	Intellectually stimulating discussions, projects
Personal development	

Spirit

Listening to music	Spending time with friends and family
Meditation	
Prayer	Spending time in nature
Reflection	Laughter

We've all heard of the golden rule, "Do unto others as you would have them do unto you." This rule teaches us to treat others in a way that we would want to be treated. The commandment, "Love thy neighbor as thyself," implies that you love yourself first in order to share that love with others. In learning to put yourself first and treat yourself with honor and love, you must "do unto *yourself* as you would do for others." This means you treat yourself as well as you would treat any other person.

A Walk Through the Clouds: The Inner Critic

"It is easy to shield our bodies against poisoned arrows from without but difficult to shield our minds against poisoned darts from within."
—Buddha

One of the most powerful forces you have is your inner dialogue. All day long, you are talking and listening to yourself. There is a conversation going on in your head. What is it saying to you?

Pay attention to this voice. Each of us has an inner critic that says all sorts of negative and horrible things about ourselves. The inner critic is full of judgment and blame. It's strong and forceful and is part of our human experience.

The inner critic can be a voice that reminds you of someone in your life. It can take on a persona from someone you know. It thrives and grows from negativity in your life and feeds off your feelings of low self-worth. It doesn't want you to succeed. It wants you to stay needy and under its control. It is allied with your ego and prefers the status quo, even if the status quo isn't good for you. It detests change.

Your inner critic will say things to you that you would never say to another person. You will think things about yourself so horrible that you would never repeat them to anyone nor would you ever want people to find out that you think these thoughts.

You are not alone. Each of us has a mind that will tell us we are no good, not worth anything, a failure....The trick, you see, is to recognize that these thoughts are not real. And you have the power to think differently.

What we think about we bring about. If you are telling yourself all day long that you're worthless and no good, then you are reinforcing that with your behaviors and you begin acting like someone who doesn't care about themselves. Your inner dialogue impacts your life. Learning to honor yourself starts with gaining control over your most important ally—your mind.

COACHING TIP: You are more powerful than these thoughts! You have the power to simply notice them. This is the power of awareness. When you start to become aware of these negative thoughts, simply choose to not listen. "Thank you for sharing but I'm not interested right now."

You can challenge their validity: What are the facts—what is true? You are not the worst person in the world. You have every right to do what you want. Find a reference in your life to prove it wrong. Think of a time when you were successful, you did follow through, or your presence was meaningful in the life of another.

Whenever you think something negative, become aware of it and then simply change it to something positive. "I'm not ugly. I am a child of the universe and I do everything to look my best." You are what you think about all day long. Choose your thoughts wisely. Make a short list of characteristics or qualities you want to develop and carry them with you. Whenever you have a negative thought, respond to it by reading the list and telling yourself this is what you are. "I'm not mean. I am supportive, attentive, and a good listener."

The best way to stunt your inner critic's growth is to eliminate all negative people and conversations, do not allow or permit yourself to think anything negative. Simply catch those negative thoughts and do not entertain them. They are not real.

You are an incredible and powerful individual. You are a gift to this world and you do not have the right to put yourself down—even in the privacy of your own mind.

Learning to put yourself first means accepting responsibility for your life. Personal responsibility means that you accept the state of your life as it is now and forever more. It means that you are responsible for your life, your choices, and your happiness. The moment you accept your life as it is, right now, is when you free yourself. You free yourself from the victim role, from excuses of how things got to be the way they are, from blaming someone else for getting you here, from believing that something outside you will "fix" things. When you accept your life as it is—like it or not—it frees you to change it. Until you can accept it, you are not at choice. You just keep going and going, much like the Energizer bunny, hoping and wishing for something to change but without accessing the power to do anything to create the change.

You have a tremendous amount of power within you. You are *not* a victim of circumstance. Things happen in life and when you look at those situations, you ask the question, "How am I responsible? *Who am I being* that has brought this into my life? What is there to be learned from this experience?" Sometimes there are lessons you may not want to learn, but they are given to you whether you want them or not. You merely need to learn to accept what is and be open to learn the lessons as they are presented to you.

Often you cannot control circumstances and events that happen in life, but you can control who you are and how you show up. You can experience peace within you as you stand in the midst of chaos and face life's challenges with a style and grace that demonstrates your inner fortitude and confidence.

When you accept responsibility, you stop resisting what is and start living your life knowing that the universe has its reasons for things. You stop trying to change what you have no control over and focus instead on what you can control—*you*. Accepting responsibility means freeing yourself from blaming others or living in the victim role, and instead changing your framework to empower yourself to do what *you* need to do—what you *can* do—to achieve the results you seek.

When you accept responsibility, you empower yourself. It means that you have power over your life and you can choose to make different choices to chart a new course. You are responsible for the direction of your life. It's very liberating—even if you don't like the state of your life!

What would it be like if you started to put yourself first? How would things be different? What wonderful things would you do for yourself each day? What would it take for you to accept responsibility for your life and to give yourself permission to become the most important person in your life? Take a moment right now to make a personal vow to honor yourself in every way. This is a journey; it's about progress, not perfection. Thank yourself for the gift you have just given to the most important person in your life.

Speaking Highly of You

There are several ways to honor yourself. You honor yourself when you learn to treat yourself with respect and love. One way to do this is to never speak negatively about yourself. We just discussed how you talk *to* yourself about yourself; it's also never acceptable to put yourself down to others. When you were young, your mother taught you, "If you don't have anything nice to say, don't say anything at all." Well, this applies to you as well! Take care in speaking about yourself. Never say anything negative. This damages your Inner Self and your self-confidence. What you say about you and what you think about you, become a self-fulfilling prophesy. Choose your words wisely.

COACHING NOTE: Self-Esteem

How you think about yourself is irrelevant when it comes to self-respect and self-love. Honoring yourself does not require self-esteem. Self-esteem is how you think of you. You are limited by how you think about yourself. The fact is it doesn't matter what you think of you. Your job in this lifetime is to be who you are capable of being. You are a gift to the world. You don't have the right to hold back for any reason.

You are who you are. How you think about yourself is a judgment you don't have the right to make unless you're using that judgment as an impetus for change.

You are a child of the universe, a part of nature just like the trees and the flowers, the bees and the lions. You have a right to be here. And you have gifts and talents and strengths that are part of you. You are meant to discover and maximize those gifts. Stop thinking about how you think of you and just be you; simply start honoring yourself and treating yourself with respect. Focus your energies on discovering and developing yourself rather than focusing on or trying to change how you think about yourself. As you move forward in becoming the person you were meant to be, you will automatically think differently about yourself. You will move beyond judgment and into gratitude.

If there is something you don't like about yourself, then either come to terms with it or fix it in a way that suits you. My client Laura remarked, "I hate my thighs. They just seem too big for my body." Laura enjoys running. I asked her, "Do your legs work well? Are you able to run as fast and as far as you'd like?" She got the message.

If her legs were skinnier, it's possible they would not be as effective. The point is that she was blessed with two legs that worked perfectly well at carrying her the way she enjoyed. She had no right to criticize; she needed to learn to be grateful. It's about learning to come from a different perspective—remembering what's really important.

"Who you are" is not what you think of you. What you think about yourself and what you are doing and being are separate. There is a capacity of who you are capable of becoming; instead of worrying about what you think of yourself, focus your attention on maximizing your capacity. This is honoring yourself.

Anytime you accidentally say something negative about yourself, whisper a small apology to yourself. This demonstrates self-respect, a caring, and a concern for your Inner Self. By focusing on speaking highly of yourself, over time, you'll find yourself moving out of the negative habit of putting yourself down.

And speaking of apologies, only apologize for things that you are responsible for. Apologizing unnecessarily is disrespectful. It also sends the impression that you are accepting responsibility for things over which you have no control. "I'm so sorry that it's raining today." Why are you sorry? You cannot control the weather!

The language you use matters. There is always an impact. It must be treated with care. This is why communicating is a personal power. Learning to speak the truth means first you must become aware of it; you must be open to explore the truth. Powerful communication is advanced personal development. Being grounded in who you are is a prerequisite for being a powerful communicator. It requires a high level of personal awareness, emotional intelligence, and openness. Think of personal development as a continuum; there are many levels and people are at different points on the continuum. As you continue on your personal *Journey Called YOU*, you'll evolve on your path of development and you'll learn to speak your truth.

Saying Yes to You

You honor yourself when you say "no" to the things you don't want. When you start saying "no" to things that are not the best use of your time or that do not bring you joy and happiness, you are saying "yes" to you! When you learn to honor yourself, you start taking yourself more seriously. Trivial things become important if they are not in your best interest.

Every time you say "yes" to a request when you'd rather say "no," makes a statement to your Inner Self that you do not matter or that others matter more than you. Over time, this translates into poor self-esteem.

Also, when you say "yes," but you want to say "no," you wind up spending your time doing things that don't make you happy or that take you away from what you could be doing. This results in an opportunity cost. There is a cost whenever you make one choice over another. If you make a choice to do something you want to do, there is no loss since you are happy with your choice. You are living exactly the way you want at this moment.

When you do not honor yourself and choose to do what another wants of you over what you want for yourself, then there is a cost or loss to you since what you really want to be doing you're not doing. Although others may not like it when you say "no," you are not responsible for their happiness. You are only responsible for your own.

Learning to say "no" clears the way for you to say "yes" to things you do want. You may find that you don't know what you want. That's okay. By clearing the way, you create space. Being in that space might feel boring at first, but after a while you will learn to protect it. Eventually you will start adding only those things that bring you joy and you'll start having more fun in your life. You may not know how to have fun—perhaps you never learned what fun is for you as an adult. This is your life journey; go discover what fun looks like for you. Certainly, do not fill your time with wasteful busyness just because you don't know what else to do to make yourself happy. Give yourself permission to do nothing. Take a walk. Write in your journal. Be with nature. Spend time alone. Eventually, things will become clearer to you.

Learning to feel comfortable saying "no" will take some time. Say it anyway. If something doesn't bring you joy or add to your life in some way, then it's depleting you. Give yourself permission to only do those things that bring you joy and add to your life.

Raising Your Standards

"Don't lower your expectations to meet your performance. Raise your level of performance to meet your expectations. Expect the best of yourself, and then do what is necessary to make it a reality."
—Ralph Marston, author of *The Daily Motivator*

You honor yourself when you eliminate anything from your life that is not good for you or that does not meet your standards for excellence.

We all learn to settle for things in life. In your early adult years, you're really just learning how to live. Everything is a new experience and you may not question whether it is good enough or not good enough. You pass them off by simply saying to yourself, "This is just the way it is." Or perhaps you just don't know that things can be better, or you don't know how to make them better. Perhaps you simply never considered what excellence would be like.

Over time, you learn to put up with so much that is less than what you would consider excellent. You may not know you have a choice. There's always a choice. This is where your power is. When things seem to be at their worst, look for your choices. Often the most horrible problems can be approached with a new perspective or attitude. In every problem, there is a rich lesson. Learn the lesson so it doesn't repeat itself in another way. And take a wider view so you can see where this might lead you in your life.

You deserve excellence—whatever that looks like for you. Awaken yourself to the possibilities of what excellence looks like in all areas of your life. Envision what you want to have in your life. Be more aware of where mediocrity shows up versus excellence. Choose to spend your time in excellence.

There are two focuses here: First, eliminate anything less than excellent, and second, define what excellence means for you. Identify all of the things you are putting up with and list them on a sheet of paper. You may find fifty or a hundred things, people, or situations that you are tolerating in your life, career, relationships, body, environment, and finances. Just by listing them, you create a new level of awareness and an inner shift occurs. This is a powerful lesson in awareness. It's not an opportunity to beat yourself up by telling yourself, "Look at all the things that are substandard in my life!" Rather, it's a starting point for you to learn to never tolerate anything that is less than what you want it to be.

Eliminate everything on your list, one at a time. It may take years to get rid of things you've been putting up with, either by eliminating them or creating a plan of action to make things the way you want. But in the process, you will learn to no longer tolerate less than excellent. You will create a mindset to stop accepting things in your life that are less than what you really want, raising your standards. It also creates space. As you eliminate what you don't want and what doesn't bring you joy, you have the space to bring in only those things that are fabulous.

An example would be cleaning out your closets of any and all clothes that do not fit just the way you want them to. All of those shoes you have but you never wear because of the blisters they cause, give them to charity. Someone else will enjoy those shoes. Someone else really needs that outfit you never wear. This is how you create a flow of energy in the universe. Things are not meant to remain stagnant and unused. By holding onto things you don't need or want, you send a clear message to the universe that you are closed or that the energy that enters will become bottlenecked with you. Energy wants to stay in motion; it doesn't want to remain stagnant.

Enjoy what you own and when you stop enjoying it, do something to fix it or pass it on to someone else who will find joy in it. In doing so you not only honor yourself, but you honor others. And once you've created space, give yourself permission to only wear clothes that make you look and feel wonderful. When you purchase new clothes, be sure to buy only those items that are of excellent quality and fit. And if they don't meet your new standard, return them or keep your money in your pocket.

You need to know what excellence looks like and how it feels in order to know it when it happens. Good enough is not excellence. If something is just good enough, it's probably not. You know when you receive mediocre service at a restaurant versus when the service is excellent. Start paying attention to what feels exceptional.

Teaching Others to Honor You

You honor yourself when you teach other people how to treat you with respect.

Personal boundaries are the limits you set for how others may act or speak in your presence. They are lines you draw that define yourself. They are not walls to shut people out, rather limits that keep the unwanted behaviors of others from entering your space. Boundaries are essential for personal health. They act as filters, permitting what's acceptable into your life and keeping other elements out. Your boundaries are about what others may do to you or in your presence.

Whenever you are in a situation that's uncomfortable, it's imperative that you speak up; the person needs to know that the behavior is inappropriate and that you will not tolerate it. When you say nothing, the impact is great—to both you and the other person. Saying nothing sends the message that the behavior is acceptable, and the person is more likely to repeat it. Others may interpret this to mean that it's okay to act in that way. Saying nothing can also leave you feeling victimized.

Learning to assert yourself in a way that gets your point across with grace and style is part of your personal development; it takes some tools, a little practice, and a lot of courage. Becoming assertive will build your leadership muscles and foster self-respect, as well as decrease your level of stress.

Whatever offenders do, you must remember that it's not personal; it's not about you even though it *feels* personal. Another person's behavior is always about him or her, about the thoughts he or she harbors, and about any unmet personal needs. For example, if someone raises his or her voice, swears, or speaks down to you, this person may want power or attention. Whatever the reason, it is about that person, not you.

You need to identify your boundaries. You may not know a boundary exists until someone crosses it. Ask yourself how you want to be spoken to and how you want to be treated. Take notice of your feelings. Your feelings are your inner messengers, your inner guidance system. When a boundary is crossed, there is a definite physiological response. If someone's comments or actions make you uncomfortable, notice how you react. Notice what part of your body reacts and acknowledge the feeling. Note what the person is doing or saying that is giving you this reaction and empower yourself by responding appropriately.

Once you are clear about your boundaries, you must educate people as to how to act in your presence. If you never tell anyone how to treat you, they will treat you in whatever way they choose. When you say nothing, you give your power away. When you assert your boundaries, you are telling others how you expect to be treated and you are respecting yourself.

Be direct in your communication. Tell the other person, "This doesn't work for me." These words are nonjudgmental, they do not make anyone wrong, and they clearly express your feelings. Sometimes, it's not enough to simply tell someone what doesn't work. You may need to let that person know how you expect to be treated.

You may become angry, frustrated, or sad when a boundary is crossed. Don't suppress your feelings; when you suppress your emotions, you only hurt yourself by increasing your stress and expending energy on keeping the feelings pent-up, which eventually can cause physical harm to your body. You also don't want to react inappropriately to your emotions either. Identify the source of the emotion, which is the other person's actions and your permitting it in your space, and learn how to respond appropriately to get the results you want.

A Walk Through the Clouds:
Ineffective or Nonexistent Support

"Keep away from people who try to belittle your ambitions. Small people always do that, but the really great make you feel that you, too, can become great."
—Mark Twain

Having no support is not helpful in your quest for a great life. You don't live on an island. We are social beings and require one another to assist us in finding meaning and in appreciating life.

The wrong support can be quite damaging to the spirit. These are people who tell you what to do, tell you what *they* would do if they were you, or tell you all the things you shouldn't do. There are those in your life who act like your worst enemy, telling you how you can't possibly succeed. They tell you all of the things that can go wrong, in case you hadn't already considered them. These people are vexations to your success. They are worse than your own inner critic! What purpose do they serve in your life?

Most people do not listen well and when they hear what you say, they often respond from their own perspective, meaning they tell you what they would do rather than help you to figure out your own answers. People turn the conversation around and instead of keeping the focus on you, they tell you all about their own experience. This, too, is not helpful.

Friends and family may also have their own agenda about who you should be and what you should do. If you want to discuss an exciting new goal, it's possible they will not be happy for you. They might be threatened by the possibility for your success, especially if your choices are not consistent with what they would choose for you.

Whether you are unleashing the grip of your past or setting big goals for your future, having support is imperative—the right support, that is.

COACHING TIP: Surround yourself with people who challenge you to be your best. Only elicit assistance from those individuals who provide you with unbiased support and encouragement. Having the right support for the goals you want to achieve will help you attain your goals that much quicker and easier. A masterful coach can help you here. You need not do this alone!

Being around people you enjoy, who are positive and uplifting, and who offer new perspectives add value to your life. Negative people deplete your energy. The more you evolve and develop yourself, you may find yourself outgrowing some of the people in your life. Give yourself permission to move on. Not everyone is meant to be in our lives forever. Everyone and everything is temporary; this is a lesson we must all learn about life.

Living in Integrity

You honor yourself when you live in integrity.

When you are in integrity, life flows easily. You make decisions based on what works for you and what makes you feel good. That's how to define your integrity; it's that place where you do what is right for you. No one can tell you what's right for you; you know by how you feel. If you do something that's not congruent with who you are *in integrity*, then you feel bad, you have trouble sleeping at night, and you experience an increased level of stress. Without integrity, it's impossible to have or build great things. It may look good but the effect is shallow and not sustainable. Think of a building without the proper level of support beams. It may look good but one strong wind....

Integrity is a choice. Either you want to be in integrity or you don't. Each of us has our own level of integrity; there is no universal truth. And as you evolve and grow as an individual, your integrity tightens and you'll find it more difficult to step out of alignment with your integral path without feeling very uncomfortable.

Integrity means wholeness. It is the result of being in alignment with *who you truly are*—living your values, accepting responsibility for all that occurs in your life, and being clear of what has occurred in the past. Having unresolved issues clouds your ability to determine your level of integrity. This means, you need to clear up what is costing you from your past (such as emotional issues, previous hurts or concerns, anything left unsaid). Clearing up the past means that you say what needs to be said, correct any wrongs, make the changes necessary so things work well, and fully handle the tasks you need to accomplish. There is nothing left that needs to be handled or communicated. And when something comes up, you deal with it immediately.

Laws are put into place to help us stay in integrity. Because people's levels of integrity differ, laws protect us from the lack of integrity, or wrongdoings, of others.

Living in integrity, starting to honor your own levels of right and wrong, is the very beginning of the continuum of personal development. Integrity and personal responsibility for your life is where personal development starts, and many people never get started. If you are unhappy with some aspect of your life, instead of looking outside for blame or for answers, look within at how you are living and the choices you are making that are incongruent or out of alignment with what is right for you.

Where are you out of integrity? Are you clear about your values and are your behaviors reflective of those values? In other words, if you value your family yet spend sixty hours at work each week, are you living your life grounded in your values? What do you need to be doing that you are not attending to? Wherever you are out of integrity, it gives you stress. It takes energy to maintain a facade. Make a list of the items where you are out of integrity and work to get back into integrity.

Integrity is your own inner barometer for right and wrong; when you learn to tap into your own inner wisdom, then you can use your power to make decisions that bring you the most joy and happiness. At the end of the day when you lay your head on your pillow, if you feel good about the decisions you've made and the things you said and accomplished, then you are in integrity. Those days add up and over time, you'll feel good about the course of your life. And at the end of your life, when you rest your head on your pillow for the last time, you'll feel good about the life you've lived and the choices you've made.

Integrity isn't something you do once; it is the choices you make hour by hour, day by day. Wherever you are out of integrity and not doing things that honor you, you are bringing stress to your life. Your inner voice—that internal mind chatter that continues endlessly—talks loudly when you are not in integrity with what is true for you.

As you start to make choices that put you in alignment with what is right for you, you'll notice that your mind has less to chatter about. It quiets down. It's loud because it wants you to take notice of it. And once you pay attention, acknowledge it, and then honor it, it has much less to say.

Experiencing Your Feelings

"We may miss a great deal of joy because we expect it to be unusual, dramatic, and spectacular. We are waiting for lights to flash and bells to ring. But the truth is that joy is here, right now, waiting for us to notice it."
—Veronica Ray, author of *Choosing Happiness: The Art of Living Unconditionally*

You honor yourself when you learn to acknowledge your feelings, experience them, and respond to them appropriately.

Learning to manage your feelings is probably one of the most important lessons you'll learn in life. Unfortunately, many people react to things out of habit. Your feelings are the gateway to your soul. They are the way the universe communicates to and through us. Your feelings align the mind, body, and spirit as one. Learn to access and honor your feelings and you will maximize your level of enjoyment of life as well as your connection to everything that exists.

To experience feelings is never bad. Even those feelings that are supposedly "negative" aren't bad; they just are. When you are sad or frustrated or angry, it brings your attention to something that isn't working in your life at that moment. If you resist, the feelings become amplified and you experience stress and struggle.

When you learn to feel your feelings, acknowledge them, understand where they are coming from and what they are trying to tell you, it feels good. It feels good to cry when you feel sad. It feels good to talk about it when you are frustrated. You don't always want answers; sometimes you just want to talk and be heard.

The process of experiencing and dealing with feelings is known as emotional intelligence. Emotional intelligence (EI) is the capacity to effectively perceive, express, understand, and manage your emotions and the emotions of others in a positive and productive manner. EI is about connecting with others and with yourself on an emotional level. Those that possess a high EI are more successful in relationships and are viewed as more effective leaders. As it becomes more well known and understood, EI is being introduced in schools and in corporations.

You are also emotionally intelligent when you manage the impressions or the impact you have on others when they are with you. People will remember how they feel when they are with you. This is very powerful!

You are meant to experience the full range of emotions, that's why you are blessed with them. Feelings are gateways to another level of awareness. As you become a personal observer, how you experience your feelings and how well you respond to emotions, are all pieces to the puzzle of you.

What's amazing is how many people are numb to their feelings. They are so out of touch with how they feel and consequently, they are out of touch with who they are. Perhaps they're just too busy to allow themselves to feel. When you keep busy, you miss out on the cues your body gives you. When you're moving at a hundred miles an hour, you cannot hear your body talk to you. You are apt to experience emotional reactions causing you to behave impulsively to events and people without stopping to consider what's really happening and how you really feel about the situation. You also don't choose your response when you react; rather, you react out of habit—the way you always react when something makes you feel this way.

Making the shift from someone who is emotionally reactive to someone who responds gracefully takes time and practice and effort. In order to respond rather than react, you have to stop when you feel an emotional charge and identify what you are experiencing. Stillness provides the environment for emotions to be explored. Then, you can identify what that feeling is trying to communicate to you.

You may find that when you feel something, you intellectualize about it. You try to rationalize or talk yourself out of your feelings. "I shouldn't feel sad. It's not right." You feel what you feel. Learn to allow yourself to feel whatever comes up for you. Give yourself permission to experience the full range of feelings available to you.

By avoiding your feelings, they don't just go away. They remain, if you will, in "boxes" stored for you to experience at a later time. If you permit yourself to experience whatever feelings come up for you and just sit with the feelings, they dissipate. They go away when you *feel* them.

Feelings can also be remembered by the body. When you feel something, you might try to remember a time when you've felt this before. The answer might provide you with some insight as to what's going on for you. If we know that lessons repeat and repeat, then if you can identify when you felt this way before, you can see if the lesson is the same, even though the situation is different. Perhaps you are experiencing the lesson again and because you are more open, more aware, and more knowledgeable; you are ready to learn the lesson.

A Walk Through the Clouds: Default Feelings

Often people will learn to feel one emotion so strongly that it becomes what I call their "default feeling." For men, often this is anger. Whenever you feel some emotion, it gets expressed or interpreted as anger when in fact it could be frustration, sadness, disappointment, and so on. Anger is okay. It is socially acceptable. How often do you hear people talk about their disappointment? Or their sadness? Something happens and you just get angry! Men used to be taught that it's not acceptable to cry. There are still people who live by this outdated and unfortunate rule.

Shame is another common default emotion. Whenever some feeling occurs, it is translated into shame. In this way, you are recreating the same events so as to continue to persist in a certain pattern until you learn the lesson—the lesson of your own emotions, the lesson of forgiveness.

Mastery of emotions is so important it's now an entire field of study known as emotional intelligence. Although it took only a few thousand years to get us to this place, it's a remarkable place to be. Finally, people are acknowledging the heart is just as important, if not more so, than the head. The more self-aware you are, the more you can self-regulate, and the more you can relate to and handle the feelings of others, the higher your emotional intelligence. It's all about feelings—yours and others'.

COACHING TIP: Whenever an emotion is experienced, take a moment to feel this feeling—where is it showing up in your body? What is this feeling? Describe it. When have you felt this before? Allow yourself to simply sit with it and then, let it go.

You cannot reason with, problem-solve, or rationalize with emotion. If you are emotional, you must learn to either deal with the emotion in the moment, or put it aside until you can deal with it at a safe time. You cannot think and feel at the same time. You must learn to fully experience your emotions. Process them and then respond using your intellect to bring about the results you want.

This is true with others as well. If you are in conversation with someone and they become emotional, deal with the emotion; don't avoid or ignore it. "You seem angry. Do you want to discuss that or do you need a few moments?" Allow the person to experience their emotions. They will not be rational if they are emotional because they are leading with their emotions rather than their mind. You cannot intellectualize with emotions. If the person cannot or will not deal with their emotions or separate them for the time being, then you may need to leave or your efforts at discussion will be futile.

COACHING NOTE: Without Emotional Charge

An important part of communicating is to be able to communicate without any emotional charge, also known as "charge neutral." This means that you have no emotion in your tone or words and you speak with a straight face, no facial expressions. When speaking with another, you can say anything, address any behavior, and deal with any issue if you have no emotional charge. Having no emotional charge paves the way for your being very direct and seeking the truth in conversation. It means that you have no attachment to the outcome of the conversation, you have no agenda, and you have left your ego completely out of the conversation. There is no judgment. The conversation is "pure," if you will. It is simply Truth.

Eliminating Struggle

You honor yourself when you learn to more readily accept what is and give up your wanting for things to be different.

Most pain and struggle in life is due to an unwillingness to simply allow things to be as they are. Things are exactly as they are meant to be, regardless of whether you like them or not. By wanting things to be different or by denying reality or that things have changed, people struggle. It is hard to keep up with the changes in life but the more you are able to "go with the flow" or "ride the rollercoaster of life," the easier it will be for you to adapt to those changes and to experience whatever feelings come up for you. This is the journey toward inner peace while life happens.

When you find yourself struggling or in emotional pain, ask yourself, "What am I resisting?" Resistance is the opposite of acceptance. If you are resisting, you are denying the truth and that causes struggle and stress.

What is the Truth? The Truth is *what is*, not what you *think* it is, not what you think it *should* be. It is what it is. When you stop trying to change things you have no control over—like other people, situations, events—and focus on accepting what is and exerting your power over the things you can control—yourself—you become free. You free yourself to enjoy the present moment with all the richness that exists in the now.

What are you struggling with? Are you living in the past? Are you keeping busy to avoid something? Perhaps you are struggling with the rules that you've been living under. Or perhaps you are struggling with long-held beliefs. Whatever it is, so long as you continue to struggle, you continue to feed it power. Whatever it is, just face it. The truth will set you free—free to be more of what is possible for you to become. You may not like what the truth awakens you to, but without the truth you live a lie. Can the lie possibly be better than the truth?

By continuing to struggle, you are giving your power to some force outside you. You have the power to free yourself to be you. Give yourself permission to think differently, to ask different questions, and to explore different answers—ones that suit who you are and the person you want to be.

Struggle is a choice. When bad things happen, you struggle with the pain it causes, the sadness or emptiness it brings you because you want things to be different. But you don't need to struggle. What if instead you accepted this new event in life as being the new reality? What is there for you to learn from this event? How can you expand yourself with this new landscape? You will still experience all kinds of emotions as you come to terms with this new reality. Allowing yourself to accept what is without fighting it and experiencing your feelings as they come up results in a peaceful and even enjoyable transition through the constant ebbs and flows in life.

When my dear friend and ex-husband, John, died at the age of 43, I was so sad. It was strange to have such deep outpouring of emotion for someone from whom I was divorced. I learned so much from this experience—about death, life, people, and myself. Death really is the ultimate teacher.

I choose not to struggle with his death but to accept that death is an inevitable part of life. He was at peace, and for a man who lived in chronic physical pain after numerous back surgeries, he was now out of pain. I allowed myself to grieve; what that looked like for me was to cry, be with my son and family members, and journal as much as I could so I could come to understand what this new event meant in my life.

I had known John for twelve years. We were together as a couple for seven years. And although there was a lot of "stuff" we went through together, there was also a lot of love. And that's when I realized that the pain and sadness I experienced was because there *was* love. If there were no love, there would be no sadness or pain.

We remained friends after our divorce. We had our son, Joshua, to raise. But John continued to fill a void in my life that I didn't know existed until he died. He listened to me. He was always interested in hearing how things were going and he held this wonderful place for me; it was always a place of greatness that he knew I was capable of aspiring to. He believed in me—always. And that was an incredible feeling.

It is often difficult for us to see our own greatness without knowing that someone else believes in us and sees something in us that we may not yet be able to see. I now hold that place of greatness for others—for *you*. And my life and my work are dedicated to creating an environment that includes a safe place without judgment, and to providing education and guidance in order to unleash the greatness of you.

The reality of life without John in the physical world awakened me to the realization that I was living without a strong community of support. I would need to take the time and energy to make new friends, build new relationships, and create a community to help raise our son.

During this time of grieving, I awakened to how others handle death. When they heard of John's death, some people avoided me. People often didn't know what to say. Sometimes people would change the subject. I didn't take this personally. I was able to handle my grief, to cry alone. But I was interested in what that meant for *them*.

I learned that people have difficulty with the subject of death because when someone dies they think of their own mortality. They can't deal with the fact that someday they, too, will die. They have not yet accepted the impermanence of all things.

Another thing I noticed is that people feel that they should do something or say something to the grieving person, and because they don't know what to do or say, they avoid them. The fact is that when people are grieving, they just want to grieve, whatever that looks like for them. They want to cry and not have to suppress their feelings. People need to process their feelings—to feel the feelings and to talk about them. If someone you know experiences a death or loss, just be with them. You don't need to do anything; just let them know that you care. If you experience a loss, give yourself permission to feel your feelings and to talk about what you feel with a supportive person.

Death forces us to look at how we are living. Are we happy? Are we living this life in the way we want? Is there anything missing? If you found out you were going to die in six months, how would you spend your time? How different would that look from how you live now?

The solution? Focus on living each day to the fullest. If you are not living in a way that makes you happy, do something about it. Face everything. Whatever it is, the lesson will show up again in other ways until you "get" the lesson. *You* go with you everywhere you go; you cannot hide from yourself. Hence, what you resist persists. If you live as if today is the most important day of your life, there will be no regrets when your time is up.

About six months before his death, John moved to Florida, something he had always talked about. Shortly after he moved, I phoned him to thank him for the role he played in my life. I realized how much he meant to my personal development throughout the years we were together. Without his love and persistent support, it would have been a much longer, more challenging, and lonely road. John was a very humble man and at first, he shrugged me off; like most people, he had difficulty receiving positive feedback about who he was. But I needed him to hear me. I needed for him to know how I appreciated him and what he meant to me. I made sure he heard the words and that he "got" the meaning of those words. When he started to cry, I knew he heard me.

Then one night a few months later, he went to bed and didn't awaken. It feels good to know that there was nothing left unsaid between us.

Going through the grief process felt good. Yes, it was hard to lose someone so close. But it felt good to cry. It feels good to miss him sometimes. It feels good to remember him with my son. What we often don't realize is that when we feel, and feel deeply, it makes us know we are alive.

A Walk Through the Clouds: The Square Peg in the Round Hole

Whenever you feel as though you are pushing, when you feel as though you are trying to fit the square peg in a round hole, recognize how you are struggling. You are forcing yourself on something—you are forcing your will, trying to gain control over something where you have none, or not accepting reality as it is. Stop pushing. Pushing is stressful. Struggle is stressful. And life is not meant to be stressful.

COACHING TIP: Relax and know that the universe is unfolding as it should. Trust that without your pushing, things will work out the way they are supposed to—not necessarily the way you want them to. Do not judge it. Just allow life to happen and watch the beauty that is. If you're feeling like you are a square peg then go look for a square hole. Knowing and accepting who you are helps you to see that your environment simply doesn't suit you. It is what it is. When you stop trying to make yourself fit into it, you free yourself to be who you are and you can discover what environment fits you best.

Creating Space

You honor yourself when you learn to clear away the clutter or baggage from your past and learn to deal with anything that comes up for you in the moment so no more clutter accumulates.

Feelings are not things to be avoided or ignored; feelings let you know you are alive. You seek out activities to make you feel good, such as sports, dancing, theater, games, or movies. You listen to music because it makes you feel. Sometimes you listen to sad music because it feels good to know that others have felt what you are feeling. And when you are sad, sometimes it feels good to just be sad. Feeling is a good thing!

But people often don't know what to do with their feelings so they avoid feeling them in the moment and, similar to clutter, they "box" their feelings for storage, to be dealt with at a later time. Clutter is just delayed decision-making. What do you do when you don't know what to do with something? Just box it up, put it away somewhere, and look at it later.

Emotion is "energy in motion." Its natural state is to move, not to stay still. When you put off dealing with your feelings, the emotional energy associated with those feelings is stored in the cells of your body, just like boxes in storage.

But what happens when you collect too much stuff? Your closets fill, your attic overflows, and you go rent a storage unit or buy a bigger house. Right?

Well, when it comes to the body, eventually you run out of space. There's no room for storing more feelings. Something gives. Usually, it's the body. There has been growing evidence linking how people live—attitudes, behaviors, reactions—with certain health concerns including cancers, heart disease, thyroid problems, and so on. When you live with unfinished business, you provide a breeding ground for the physical manifestation of disease. If you do not heed your feelings—your inner voice—then it speaks to you louder through your body. Why wait until you become ill? Learn to deal with the old feelings, put the past behind you, and then you can learn to live in the moment and clear things as they come up. You'll be lighter, freer, and your life will become simpler.

Clearing up the past is similar to clearing out an attic; it takes one box at a time. And it takes quite a while to get through each box. You have to choose a box, look through it, and decide how to deal with it.

The only way is to tackle it head-on. You must face whatever emotional energy you still carry and store from your past. As long as you hold onto it, it holds you captive and takes up space. You cannot change the past. You simply need to accept it as it was and learn from it. You learn to accept what is. The only person you hurt by still trying to change the past and by continuing to harbor anger or some other emotion, is you. And by continuing to expend energy to hold onto the past, you are avoiding the present.

As soon as you feel the feeling you've had bottled up all this time, you'll feel its power over you dissipate. You'll realize that feeling your feelings feels good. It's freeing.

By keeping storage boxes of old stuff, you are unable to truly enjoy today. As you clear away the old feelings and release the boxed-up emotional energy, you create space for you to be fully present in the moment. This allows you to feel deeply in the moment and to enjoy your feelings—whatever they happen to be. When you feel deeply, you experience the richness of being human.

EXERCISE: "Squeezing the Lesson"—Integrating the Lessons of the Past

Spend some time writing your life story in your journal. Don't worry about punctuation, grammar, or margins. Just write. Let your mind flow. The purpose is to allow yourself to revisit things and people in your life that made an impression. Then you can evaluate that impression and determine whether it benefits you or if perhaps the meaning you assigned to this person or event was incorrect or misguided. You get to choose how the person or event impacts you today. You can accept the person or event for what it was in your life: a lesson to be learned. And if there is still an emotional charge when you think about this person or thing, then you can identify the feelings you've attached to this and feel them so they no longer have a controlling hold on you and your life.

The people in our lives are with us for only a time. Everything and everyone is temporary. Some people will stay with us for many years, others only a short while. Events, too, are passing and are rich with lessons for you to learn. If the thought of the person or event still holds an emotional charge, then perhaps you missed the lesson. Now is the time to look back into your past and learn those lessons so you can move forward. As long as there is a charge and the lesson has yet to be learned, the lesson will repeat in different ways until you finally "get" it. Why not learn all you can now? I call this "squeezing the lesson," just like "squeezing the lemon." You squeeze all you can out of each event or feeling so you can learn the lesson and move beyond it.

As you look back over the years, see what events, situations, or people come up for you. But don't write about what happened—don't tell the "story." Instead, write about you—who you were and how you felt about what was happening. Then consider how your interpretation of the event supports or impacts you today. Is there anything you can learn from this event considering that time has passed and you are coming from a different perspective? How has the experience of this event added to your life?

Regardless of what happened, the story is just a story. There are no mistakes in life; things happen for a reason even if we don't know what those reasons are. In order to truly move on, you must be willing to let go of your attachment to the story. You are not a "what." You are not what happened to you. What you learned from your experiences has helped to shape the person you are today. What do you want the experience to mean to your life? If you look at every experience as a lesson, what was this experience meant to teach you?

COACHING TIP: This is a lesson of letting go. Part of this exercise is to go back to your past and completely integrate all of your experiences. In doing so, you squeeze the lessons from all that you have seen, experienced, and felt.

People tend to live their present talking or focusing on the past; some live their lives reliving their past ("Ah, the good old days."). This exercise, if completed thoroughly, will bring a peace to your past. And you can fully move into the present of today.

How do you know you are complete with your past? When there is nothing you cannot talk about or think about from your past that hurts or brings up emotions. There are no more secrets. Nothing is hidden—everything is out in the open. It just happened. It's just a story. And today is a new day.

It's Not Personal

"Personal importance, or taking things personally, is the maximum expression of selfishness because we make the assumption that everything is about 'me.' During the period of our education, or our domestication, we learn to take everything personally. We think we are responsible for everything. Me, me, me, always me!"
—Don Miguel Ruiz, author of *The Four Agreements*

You honor yourself when you learn to stop taking things personally and maintain an open mindset where possibilities and opportunities for learning are abundant.

When events occur in your life, you assign meaning to them. It's part of what we do as humans. It's part of Club Human. Coming to realize that the meaning you assign may be erroneous and ineffective is helpful in order to move beyond the event.

The fact is things happen. When a hurricane strikes and your home is damaged, it's not personal. It just happens. It may have meaning for you and the course your life takes; you have to relocate, rebuild, and so on. But what does it mean in the overall scheme of life? It's just a natural phenomenon offering you an opportunity to experience and learn from. There is no "why"; it just is.

And that's what life is, an experience. You are here to experience and learn what life as a human is all about. There is nothing personal about the events in your life.

This little fact makes life so much easier to handle. When someone yells at you, it's not about you. It's about them. That doesn't mean you don't tell them to stop. *That's* about you, your boundaries, and your ability to stand up for yourself.

This is an important lesson. The sooner you understand that people do what they do and it has nothing to do with you, the sooner you discover your power. If you are busy trying to debate someone from the perspective that it's about you, you increase stress for you and the other person thinks you're paranoid. Even if the person is blaming you, it's not about you. It's about their need to be right or be in control. Blaming always means not accepting responsibility. It feels bad and it feels personal. But if you try to deal with someone on this level, you won't get the results you seek.

If you maintain your focus on what needs to be done—on results—and come from a place of mind that nothing is personal, then you'll have the power to handle any situation gracefully.

Your boss walks by and doesn't acknowledge you. "She hates me," is the thought that goes through you mind. Well, any number of things could be going through her mind. Perhaps she had an argument with her husband that morning or she just got out of a meeting with her boss and she needs to terminate an employee. For the next hour, you can waste your time and energy thinking about why she didn't say hello, or you can simply trust that it's not about you. Even if she doesn't like you, it's about *her* and who *she* is; it's not about *who you are*.

We are mirrors for one another so when you find something bothersome about another person, it's a great opportunity to explore what that is for you. What is it about that person that annoys you or gets under your skin? This is another piece of the puzzle of you. It's an opportunity for increased awareness. If you know what disturbs you, then you can own it; it's about you, not about them.

A Walk Through the Clouds: Taking Things Personally

When you take things personally, you think that everything is about you. You might even sound a bit paranoid, worrying about what others think or that other people blame you, or feeling guilty and blaming yourself for things.

The person who takes things personally often asks, "Why me?" thinking that things happen to them purposely. People do things, often bad things, to hurt other people—intentionally or not. It's about that person and who they are, where they are in their personal development, their level of awareness and understanding, and who they are choosing to be at the moment. You happen to be a target. Perhaps you are available or because of your level of awareness, you don't see it coming. But if you are attracting negative things into your life, it's an opportunity to ask yourself what you are doing in order to attract that into your life. What lesson is being presented to you? How might you need to change in order to bring about different results? Accept responsibility for what happens in your life and you'll tap into your power to change your life.

COACHING TIP: Nothing is personal. When things occur to you, don't ask "why"; instead ask yourself what you can learn. What is this event meant to teach you? There is a reason this lesson presented itself now. Explore alternative perspectives or understandings for this happening right now. Often it's exactly what you don't want to learn or face but deep down you know this is something you need to change. Maybe the lesson being offered is about slowing down or learning patience. Maybe it's about extending your boundaries and learning to stand up for yourself. By taking a thorough assessment of your life, yourself, and the situation, you increase your level of awareness which gives you the power you need to make better choices in the future. You will grow from the experience. If you take it personally, you will remain closed to the lesson. And, as you already know, the lesson will repeat itself until you learn it.

Gratitude

> "Gratitude makes sense of our past, brings peace for today, and creates a vision for tomorrow."
> —Melody Beattie, author of *Codependent No More*

There is nothing that will make you feel good about life and about living more than developing an attitude of gratitude. To honor yourself means to become thankful for each day and for everything you have to enjoy during your time here on this planet.

You are amazing! You are this spiritual being here in this body at this time in order to experience this lifetime. Isn't that incredible? You have this body for your use. You have hands and feet and muscles to make you move. You have organs and a circulatory system to keep you alive. You have a brain to think, eyes to see, and ears to hear. Every day you awaken, you are given a gift—*the gift of life!*

This is called gratitude. It's learning to be grateful for the incredible things to enjoy and experience during your time here. Perhaps you are grateful for the sun and breeze that gently touches your cheek. This means you have the sense of touch, the ability to feel warm and wind—you were given the gift of the senses in order for you to experience what exists. We access information in our environment through our senses. Learning to be grateful for the little things will create a shift in you that moves you from critical to appreciative and from what is outside you—the breeze and the sun—to what is inside you or part of you—your skin and senses and your sense of wonder.

Each of us will experience the breakdown of our body in some way. This offers us the opportunity to experience the world from a new perspective and learn to appreciate the physical gift we were given to explore the world. And although we may not want or welcome this new opportunity, everything we get is just an opportunity to explore ourselves. It simply is; judging it as good or bad doesn't make it go away.

When you come from a place of gratitude, your perspective changes and you see the world from a different viewpoint. Your values become clearer. Things that seemed important are no longer priorities and trivial things that seemed urgent can wait. Other things that seemed trivial or things you take for granted become more urgent.

An attitude of gratitude allows everything to enter—it leaves nothing out because everything is a learning experience. You can learn to be grateful for the worst lessons you experienced and know that in that experience you have grown and learned and became stronger because of the experience. You may not have chosen to suffer some physical affliction or be fired or have someone close to you die, but whatever the experience, you got through it and by simply going through it, you learned something and you are stronger because of the experience. That learning accumulates over time and no one and nothing can take that away from you. That learning is precious.

One thing that most of us don't do well is celebrate ourselves and our accomplishments. You do many wonderful things every day. You help someone meet a goal, give a compliment, hold a door—there's a thousand little things to celebrate! Make a conscious effort to celebrate you, life, and the people who share your life.

Learning to see what you have, rather than focusing on what is wrong or not quite right, is where gratitude comes in. When you learn to be grateful, you see beyond the little irritating things and realize that *all life is* can be found in this very moment. This moment is all you have. How you are spending it, is up to you. You can spend this moment being scared or worried about what might happen in the future, or be angry about something that happened in the past, or you can allow yourself to be fully present and experience the beauty that exists in this moment.

When you learn to honor yourself, you honor others. When you focus your energies on self-respect, self-love, and making choices that honor you, you naturally treat others with that same level of respect. To do otherwise would be disrespectful to you. And if you are disrespectful to you, you cannot truly respect others.

In the next chapter, "Living the Journey," we pull together how getting to know yourself at deeper and deeper levels, accepting what is, and honoring yourself, creates a life path that's fulfilling, authentic, and awesome.

Coaching Challenge

- Where are you struggling? What are you resisting?
- Where are you out of integrity? Conduct a self-assessment each day before you go to bed. What do you need to do to move yourself into integrity?
- What situation, person, or thing is most frustrating you right now? What do you need to do to honor yourself? What do you need to say "no" to?
- Start paying attention to your feelings as you go through the day. Jot them down in a notebook if you like and journal about them. Notice how your feelings come and go. And notice how you respond to them. Are you in control or do your emotions take over? Do you allow yourself to feel them?
- What are you most grateful for? Start creating a gratitude list and add three new things each day. Make sure that at least one thing is about who you are.

Chapter Eight

Living the Journey

"Peace comes within the souls of men when they realize their relationship, their oneness with the universe, and all its powers, and when they realize that at the center of the universe dwells God, and that this center is really everywhere, it is within each of us."
—Black Elk, Native American

There's this place where you come to where you feel content. There is no pressure to perform. There is no stress over which choice to make; you are just you. Things happen around you and you just deal with what's in front of you; you don't become all seduced and crazed by them. It's as if you're able to step back and look at things from this new perspective. You separate your feelings from those of others; you don't react to others. You remain calm because you're not taking things personally. It's a very peaceful place to be.

And it's a very powerful place to be.

It feels good to know who you are and to separate you from others and from the circumstances around you. You are responsible for you. You stop taking on projects that are not the best use of your time. You also learn to say "no" to the behaviors and the words of others that don't feel good for you. By treating yourself with respect, you receive greater respect from others.

160

As you grow and evolve, you naturally hold the place of greatness for others to aspire to. They will either be attracted to that or they won't. There is no judgment. Remember, we have all been at that place where our ego's pride got in the way. Or our fear. You now come from a place of love for everyone because there is no reason not to. People are wonderful, although their *behaviors* may not always be wonderful. And you are now able to separate the person from their actions, holding compassion for "who they are" and asking them to accept responsibility for their actions and the impact those actions have on others.

People are right where they are supposed to be developmentally. It is not for us to judge where others are on the personal development continuum. There's no predetermined path. You simply hold that place for others to aspire to be better.

As you figure out this "life stuff," you want to share it with the world. You want so much for others to "get it" too. They will only "get it" when they are ready to do their own inner work. And they may not be ready in this lifetime.

In this chapter, you'll read some quotes from clients who have traveled the path of *The Journey Called YOU* through our coaching together. It's amazing to see someone start to blossom and become more of themselves—to let more of *who they are* out. There's a confidence that builds over time. First, an awareness, then a feeling of power ("I can do this"), then your confidence builds. You stop looking for yourself in the eyes of others and start looking inward to find your own Truth. At some point, you burst forth and a new you emerges—it's not really "new"; it's been there all along, it just was hiding behind all of the clouds. You feel good about who you are. You possess a new energy about you. You begin to feel grounded in who you are. Choices become easier. You allow yourself to feel more deeply and more often. There's a sense of pride in being who you really are and it becomes easier to honor yourself in all you do. It's a wonderful thing to experience.

Client Comments:

"I'm nervous about all of the good things starting to happen to me. I am so used to all of the craziness. It's like giving up an abusive relationship for a healthy one. It's so easy to want to run back to it because it's familiar. But I'm going to keep pushing. It's scary because of all I have to leave behind. I want to help others see this! But they're not always ready to do what it takes to move beyond. I know that. People gain something by continuing to live in

this way. My responsibility is to be my best and be a role model for others to find their way. I feel myself growing and changing on the inside. I feel a growing strengthened sense of self. I am starting to honor myself."

Getting Out of Your Head

"If we listened to our intellect, we'd never have a love affair. We'd never have a friendship. We'd never go into business, because we'd be cynical. Well, that's nonsense. You've got to jump off cliffs all the time and build your wings on the way down."
—Ray Bradbury, American science fiction writer

Slowing down your pace and shifting your priorities clears space in your brain so your mind has less to chatter about. For a civilization so dependent on the mind and thinking, this is really important. All through school we're taught how to think, to use our brains to produce great things. No one teaches us how to *feel* and how to trust our bodies or our "gut." It's fluff. And yet, it's essential.

There is a difference between thinking about something and knowing something. When you are able to tap into your higher consciousness—your sense of knowing—then you are able to make decisions that honor you. Your logic isn't always the best judge of a situation. And yet, we are taught to honor our logic above all else.

For example, the other day I bought a new videocassette tape rewinder, a machine that rewinds tapes so you don't ruin your VCR. (I know everything is going DVD, but I still have loads of tapes!) Mine had recently stopped working. I asked my son, Josh, to grab one off the shelf. He picked up the first one in the row. Now there were several on the shelf—maybe seven—and I had an intuitive hit that told me "have him pick the third one in, not the first." This made no logical sense to me. They're all the same. What's the difference? So I ignored it. I should have known better.

I get home, unpack the box, and rewind a tape. It makes an incredibly loud noise while rewinding. I took it back and got another one. The new one was perfectly quiet as it rewound a tape.

This is a simple example, but the fact is we receive intuitive hits all of the time; when you think of someone you haven't spoken to in a while and suddenly the phone rings and it's them. Paying attention to them and then acting on them, takes awareness and practice. It also takes a lot of trust—trust in the unknown, trust in what doesn't make sense in the moment, and trust in yourself, and in your knowing or your ability to access the knowing.

This knowing—your intuition—is actually accessing a higher consciousness, the interconnectedness of everything, all knowledge and knowing. This is also called the Divine. The connection to all knowing exists within us so each of us is able to access or tap into it. You won't hear your intuition speak to you unless you pay attention. And you can't pay attention nor can you hear it when you're going a hundred miles an hour!

Intuition is accessed through the stillness of the mind. When the mind is quiet and still, only then can you access intuition. You experience your intuitive hits from somewhere else in your body, not your mind. It just comes up. For each person it's different. For me, it just comes up and I know it or I see it. And when I see it, I either trust it or I don't. I am learning to trust it more. As with the videotape rewinder, sometimes I let my mind make sense of it and whenever I do that, I choose logic over knowing and it's always a mistake.

Whenever you have a problem or situation and you're thinking about it, simply stop thinking about it. Trust that the answer will come and that you will *know* it to be the right path. This is huge. It is a leap of faith, a step off the cliff with the faith that you will sprout wings and fly.

And fly you will. You will soar. As you learn to trust and have faith in this higher consciousness, you let go of the control of the mind. Things aren't always logical because we haven't asked all of the "why" questions and we're not privy to all of the answers. Sometimes "why" reveals itself *after the fact* and we only know it in hindsight. Just like my rewinder, I had no way of knowing that there was a problem with it or that it was damaged. The universe sent me a message, "Don't choose that one. Choose another one." It didn't tell me "why" I should choose a different one. I didn't listen because it seemed silly at the time. And yet, had I done so, I would've saved myself a return trip to the store. And yet, had I chosen a different one, I never would have known that there was a problem with the first!

Intuition is the door to awareness within you. It enables you to make decisions based on what you know is true without thought, without reservation. It's only when you stop to question, when your mind puts its two cents in that you stop trusting yourself. The inner voice is always right. Often, you're not ready to trust it. And yet, there is great power here. Being able to trust that the answers will come when you most need them, and then act based on the direction it leads is very powerful.

How do we learn to access this power? When you live a hectic and chaotic life, it is very difficult to get to the quiet place to be able to "hear" what your body is telling you. The first step to strengthening your intuition is to simplify your life. Downshift. Breathe deeply and learn to experience the feelings of your body. In these feelings, sensations, and quietness, your soul speaks to you. Therein lies your intuition.

Being fully in tune with your feelings enables you to access and trust your intuition. Growing up, I always used the motto "when in doubt, do without." This little phrase was my way of tapping into my intuition, even though I didn't know it at the time. But what it told me was to trust myself. If I was unsure, then I needed to *not* do it, buy it, or say it. I may not have understood "why" at the time but that wasn't what mattered; I just needed to know how to act in that moment.

Whenever you face any decision and you're thinking about it, analyzing it, comparing it, writing down the pros and cons, you are in a state of *not* knowing. You are thinking. I used to hear this a lot growing up, "You think too much." I wasn't good at trusting myself or my inner knowing. As I stated previously, I wasn't grounded in Me; I didn't have a strong sense of self so it makes a lot of sense to me today looking back on my youth that I would become an intellectual. I was taught to trust my brain.

Today, I don't analyze as much in making decisions. I consider all of the alternatives and then I let it go. I wait for the answer to come. I trust it will. And I know that I will know the answer when it comes. Sometimes you just need to sit with the questions and not try to force an outcome from your intellect. Trust that the answer will emerge when you are prepared to hear it and when the universe is prepared to give it.

Peter was an amazing client who was very accomplished. He didn't, however, recognize his worth because the environment in which he worked was not encouraging and praising. In fact, he rarely received any positive feedback at all. Through our work together, he began to identify his strengths, skills, and special gifts. He began to give himself credit for all of his hard work and accomplishments. This helped him to see himself differently and make decisions that honored him and that brought joy and love into his life.

Peter also loved to read and dialogue about what he read. He was always reading, thinking, analyzing. He looked to books—authors—for answers to his questions about life. He was in a constant state of searching for his Truth from somewhere else. Peter didn't trust himself for the answers. Through our work together, we created a shift in him from fear and uncertainty, to allowing and trusting. Until he could learn to trust himself, he would never be at peace.

Integrating the Head and Heart

As an intellectual, I learned to lead with my mind. It took me years of getting to know myself and a lot of practice to learn to trust that there was access to knowledge by some method other than the mind. The mind alone was not producing the results I wanted to achieve. I felt limited by my mind.

For me the question arose with my writing. There seemed to be a missing element. Oh the articles I wrote were fine. They were always written well and were filled with useful information. But it was sometimes very difficult to get the article on paper. All that "thinking" was a lot of work! I felt like I was struggling and I was putting out too much effort. What was the missing piece?

It was love. My heart. My heart was missing. My heart was yearning to be free. It wanted to be included in my writing. Communicating is my life, my work; it's who I am and what I do. It's how I express myself. And so I let my love out. And since I've learned to merge my head with my heart, my writing has become easier, effortless, and it feels wonderful to be in that zone. Writing is where I find "flow."

Integrating your heart means putting love into your work, letting your heart out. Too many people are stiff, all brain and little emotion, afraid to demonstrate feelings out of fear of being labeled "soft." If feelings are soft, then reasoning is hard. And without a connection to your heart, your stiffness may express itself through your body in the form of physical manifestations of disease. There is always an impact in our bodies.

When you learn to connect your head with your heart, you're not eliminating your brain, your just not relying solely on your brain. When you learn to access your intuition, your higher consciousness, and your heart along with your mind, the effects are synergistic. It's amazing what heights you can reach when you learn to use more of you in your work!

For example, had I written this book with only the knowledge in my head, the words would have been empty. Because I opened my heart, you can feel the connection to me as you read through the pages of this book. Although clearly there's a lot of information here, there's also something else—universal, unconditional, genuine love. Once I made the shift to allow my heart its place in my work, it's as though the words simply came through me from some other place. I feel as though the universe used me as a vehicle to say what it wanted the world to know, speaking my words, using my strength in communicating, and telling my story to convey the message it wanted you, the reader, to hear. And for this gift, the ability to tap into this space, I am truly grateful.

Making the trip from your head to your heart has been said to be the longest distance anyone has ever traveled. You believe, you were taught, that to *feel* is to be vulnerable and vulnerability is a bad thing. But when you let your love out, you allow love to flow through you. You start taking good care of yourself, clearing up your past, and managing your emotions because you want to feel more love and connect with others, and yourself, more deeply.

It actually makes you less vulnerable because there are no more secrets; you address everything as it comes up. No one can hurt you if you have strong boundaries and accept responsibility for your feelings, thoughts, and actions. When you feel something, you handle it by acknowledging it, processing it, and then sharing it in a way that brings about the results you want in your life.

I have learned that I have the capacity to feel very deeply. I'll cry at little things sometimes simply because they touch me in a way that evokes that kind of emotion. And today, I give myself permission to feel that deeply. It's okay to experience emotional energy and to enjoy it when it occurs. Yes, there are times when crying is inappropriate— like in the boardroom or in a meeting at work. You're responsible for managing your actions in relation to the emotions you feel. But if you experience emotional energy and are simply honest about it, you demonstrate a commitment to speak your Truth and respect your Inner Self as well as respecting the other person by sharing with them the source of your expression of emotion. By letting them in, you show your humanness which, in turn, allows them to be human as well. You'll find compassion meets you on the other side. Other people have the same feelings. When you share with them, you open the doors for them to share their feelings with you.

People long to connect more deeply. And what better way to connect than to share a heartfelt emotion? We are all connected, after all. What you feel, I feel. The energy emitted from the emotion you experience within you, I will feel in me if I am not in my mind. If I am clear and open to receive you, then I will feel your pain, your pleasure, your emotion.

Client Comments:
"I feel more deeply. I cried at an email sent to me by a friend the other day. I never did that before. Then I called her to thank her and to let her know how much it meant to me. And I realized it's the little things that make up what it is we're in search of—we want to feel something. What a fun place to play!"

Being Present for What Is

"I honor the place in you where the entire universe resides. I honor the place in you of love, of light, of truth, of peace. I honor the place within you where, if you are in that place in you, and I am in that place in me, there is only one of us."
—Samy Chong, certified executive coach

The Journey Called YOU is the journey of knowing yourself, accepting what is, and honoring yourself. Each and every day, there are new feelings, new situations, new people, new visions, and new dreams. *The Journey Called YOU* doesn't ever stop. Reading this book will get you on course. It offers you a process by which to find your path to authentic living. Hopefully, you've learned to integrate your past and are in the process of eliminating anything and everything that does not bring you joy. You are identifying the rules that keep you living under a ceiling of success. You are discovering your talents, strengths, special gifts, and desires so you can move your life into living Quadrant One every day. There is a vision for success that you hold for your life that guides your choices and stretches you to express more of what exists within you. You value your time as you know that your time equals your life. No longer do you take your moments for granted.

You are learning how to process your feelings. You surrender to what is and are beginning to loosen the attachment you have with struggle and with trying to have things be *your way*. You're letting go of "wanting things to be different" and moving forward toward your vision of success with conviction and a commitment to excellence, expressing the full essence of who you are. Giving up the struggle, you allow yourself to be with what is rather than wishing it was something different. And with this, you start to feel peace.

As you move forth in your life, you feel more self-assured. Your limiting beliefs and the obstacles that block your path start to disappear; as the sun breaks through, the clouds dissipate. You can see how if you simply move forward with confidence and grace, trusting in you and in the guidance you receive from the universe, everything will be just as it will be. No more struggle, no more stress, no more fear. There is no fear because you know that there is nothing to be afraid of. Life is as it is. You have surrendered. And whatever happens, things will be just as they are meant to be—whether you like them or not.

This is only the beginning. There are deeper and deeper levels to dive into and more ceilings to break through. If the universe exists within you, then you have an entire universe to explore! Can you ever completely understand the universe? You can start by learning to master yourself. This is the essence of *The Journey Called YOU*.

Client Comments:

"I'm walking through life observing myself. Every time I feel something, I look at it. I give myself permission to sit with the feeling or I can give myself permission to let go and decide to do something to be different. Because I opened myself up to deal with the past, I'm more able to deal with stuff in the present. I still have a way to go in order to let go of feelings toward my father. I still cannot accept him and his actions. But I can separate today from the past. I'm now conscious of the dynamic in my life and how I used to treat my husband because I held all those feelings. It was as though I reacted to him through all of that old stuff. I don't do that anymore. I don't approach the present looking through my past. I stay present in the moment."

Finding Your Truth

You are so incredible. There is so much to explore and to know about you. And no one can really get close to you unless you are willing to seek and to understand your own Truth. You must be awake and alert to look for it. No one can tell you your Truth. But the Truth exists; it is revealed as you become open and aware to the wisdom within you.

You are redefining yourself every moment. What is true for you today may need to be changed tomorrow, refined, developed. Do not get attached to things staying the same. As each day passes, you grow and evolve. You read more books and take in additional information, which adds to your knowledge base and, essentially, deepens your level of understanding.

Having someone to dialogue with is essential for you to uncover your Truth and your understanding of what is. Sometimes we know that there is something not quite right. Having a discussion with someone—a trusted someone—in your life, will help you access the language and get clear about what the issue is. Having the right support in your life is essential for holding that place of greatness for you to aspire to. This can be a spouse, trusted friend, or your coach. This aspiration will help you access your Truth.

On any given day, you must learn to tap into your own inner knowing for the answers. Sometimes, you don't have the knowledge in order to identify, or language, the Truth. For instance, you may intuitively know there is something wrong with you physically, but since you're not a doctor, you don't have the medical knowledge necessary to diagnosis the problem. This doesn't mean that you just take the doctor's word as Truth; his or her words must resonate with what you know to be true for you (your intuition). Although you may not know for certain what the answer is, often patients know when what the doctor is saying doesn't quite fit. This is how you practice tapping into the intuitive knowledge of the universe. Just be aware and you will learn how to navigate this area over time.

Honor yourself as you are in the moment. Honor the wisdom that lies within you. Honor the still small voice that whispers to you, telling you what is best for you.

Client Comments:

"I feel more alive than ever. Where have I been hiding all these years? I have been living a safe life in my little house with my husband who never questioned or challenged me. I just want to dance! He hates to dance. I want to travel! He hates to travel. I see it all so clearly now. I grew up with the overwhelming need for safety and security because as a child, I had none. I created a life that brought that to me—money, a house, a car, a husband. But it wasn't Me. Where was Me in that picture? Now that I know so much more about myself, I see that I don't need something outside of me to make me safe. Safe doesn't equate to happy. And it never really did. It just made me safe and created a [self-imposed] ceiling that I lived under. I lived behind a facade that everything was all right. It looked all right to others. But I was lost. Who was I? I felt like I was running around living my life in search of. I wasn't living; I was looking. Now I have found...Me.

"I have learned that I need to free myself from my need to be protected, safe, and secure. This life may be safe, but it is very confining. I want more! I give myself permission to live where I want to live, do the things that bring me the most joy and fulfillment, and to fully express the wonderful woman that I am! Thank you for helping me to set myself free."

Faith and Trust in the Universe

"Until one is committed, there is hesitancy, the chance to draw back, always ineffectiveness. Concerning all acts of initiative and creation, there is one elementary truth the ignorance of which kills countless ideas and splendid plans: that the moment one definitely commits oneself, then providence moves too. All sorts of things occur to help one that would never otherwise have occurred. A whole stream of events issues from the decision, raising in one's favor all manner of unforeseen incidents, meetings and material assistance which no man could have dreamed would have come his way."

—W. H. Murray, from *The Scottish Himalayan Expedition*

Allow yourself to dream about the possibilities of the future. What do you want in your life? Often these dreams are sent to you through your connection to the universe. The intentions as to how you will live are not yours, per se, but were sent to you. It's the universe speaking and acting through you while you enjoy the experience of this world. In this way, your dreams and ambitions are in alignment with the universe. When this occurs, you know you are on the right course. The mind chatter is not shouting at you. Synchronistic events start to occur. Suddenly everything just seems to fall into place. Have you ever had this kind of spiritual experience?

When you are clear, when you move forward with courage and conviction, you start to see everything as synchronistic. You must learn to balance action with letting go. Your vision for the future holds the place for you to aspire to; it gives you focus and provides a beacon of light so you can move judiciously in its direction. At the same time, you must let go to allow the universe to take care of the details. The universe will fill in the gaps in knowledge or in resources. Trust that the universe will do what it needs to do to bring you closer to fulfilling your dreams. If you know you are on the right path, then you must trust that the universe will bring you what you need when you need it. If you don't have something now, then you don't need it yet. You might *think* you should have it; you might not want to wait for it. But be assured, that if it were necessary for your journey, the universe would have provided it for you.

To lead with trust and to have faith that things will work out exactly as they are supposed to, can be challenging. There's a gap between where you are and where you are heading. This gap, or "space in time," is where faith comes in. You must learn to be patient for you cannot possibly know when the universe will deliver upon its promise. It has its own time frame and we don't know what that is.

Having faith is the opposite of fear. When you have faith, you trust the unknown rather than fear the unknown. Fear and worry are fantasies. They take you out of the present and put you in the future. Fear is a dream, a nightmare. Fear is all of the things that could possibly go wrong. But the universe is never wrong. It gives you exactly what you need—the lessons you need—to move you to the next level. Whatever you fear is actually your inability to accept what is and what will be.

Death and illness, sadness and grief are never wrong or bad. They just are. And there are lessons for us to learn in all things and events and people. The universe cannot be willed to be different. It is what it is.

By learning to accept what is without attachment to what you think things should be, it's easier to handle the inevitability of change. Whatever is born, will die. Everything in the universe is temporary. The sooner you "get" this lesson, the sooner you will learn to be grateful for all that you have, for every experience, for every emotion, for every moment in time—in your life. The gift of life is to live it, enjoy it, revel in and savor each moment because that is all there is—moments of time. May you use your time wisely and enjoy every moment of *The Journey Called YOU*.

A Spiritual Experience

"To dream anything that you want to dream, that is the beauty of the human mind. To do anything that you want to do, that is the strength of the human will. To trust yourself, to test your limits, that is the courage to succeed."
—Bernard Edmonds, author

I was doing some energy work (Reiki) with a woman and during one of our sessions I had this incredible vision. I was standing on the edge of a cliff, wanting to jump off. I was ready to let go and to completely free myself. I had to take a leap of faith. And I did it. I jumped. And, I began to fly. I flew above the city and up to the clouds. It was scary at first, being so far up. But it was peaceful. It was beautiful. I felt free. I sat on a cloud and looked down, observing life from this view. I was comfortable just sitting and watching. Suddenly, a large hand reached down and lifted me up. I wasn't frightened at all. I felt complete love and acceptance. Whether you believe in God or not, you don't need to be religious to know there is a power greater than us at work in the universe. This was that power. It held me for a while and then let me go. It wanted me to fly, explore, and be free. It was as if it wanted me to know that I was not alone, rather being guided and supported by a force greater than I. I just needed to be present to it.

This spiritual experience was very enlightening for me.

Trust that things will all be all right, because they will. Trust in you because the universe resides within you and you are connected to everything in the universe. Have faith in something greater than you, because you are small in the scheme of things. And yet you matter more than you know. One life is like a ripple in still water; its impact reaches far and wide. Be free to be yourself and do what you are meant to do, because that is where your power lives.

The Journey Called YOU doesn't end here—it's just beginning. Reading this book has no doubt brought you to a much greater level of understanding of yourself, people, life, and the universe. But there are many more levels. You are hardly finished. Each day you take this same journey into exploring yourself, life, and the universe. And each day you will become more and more aware to what is. The learning never stops.

Read through the book again and again. Refer back to sections you need to review and discuss it with friends or your coach. You now have your power to chart your own course and to create a life—each day of your life—that brings you peace and joy and that allows more of you, your essence, to spring forth. The best of you is waiting, wanting you to set it free! Jump and trust that you, too, have wings and can fly; do not be afraid. I will fly with you!

About the Author

Julie Fuimano, MBA, BSN, RN, is the cofounder and chief executive officer of Nurturing Your Success, a personal and professional development company dedicated to improving the quality of life, career, finances, and work environment. She is a professional coach, a motivational speaker, and an accomplished writer.

Photo by Paula Gregorowicz

As a coach, Julie works with individual clients to help them feel more confident in their decisions, to improve their communication and leadership skills, and to increase their personal effectiveness so they can accomplish the results they want in all areas of their life, career, and relationships. She works with organizations to achieve greater productivity and improve the bottom line by providing clarity and vision, eliminating obstacles, and creating supportive environments that nurture success.

As a writer, Julie has three regular columns in healthcare journals including *Advance Newsmagazines* and *Nursing Management Journal*. Her articles appear in publications around the world and are translated into several languages. She also publishes her own electronic newsletter available through the website www.nurturingyoursuccess.com. Her presence in the marketplace extends into articles in *The Times Herald, The Morning Call,* and *Monster.com.*

Julie has a master's in business and two bachelor's degrees, and is a registered nurse. She completed her coach training through Coach University and is the 2005 President of the Philadelphia Area Coaches Alliance, the local chapter of the International Coach Federation.

Julie resides in Pennsylvania with her son, Joshua.

For information about coaching, contact her at
Julie@NurturingYourSuccess.com

Give the Gift of

The Journey Called YOU

to Your Friends and Colleagues

CHECK YOUR LEADING BOOKSTORE OR ORDER HERE

❑ **YES**, I want _____ copies of *The Journey Called YOU* at $22.95 each, plus $3.95 shipping per book. (Ohio residents please add $1.66 sales tax per book.)

Allow 15 days for delivery.
(Canadian price: $34.95)

My check or money order for $_____ is enclosed.

Please charge my: ❑ Visa   ❑ MasterCard
                    ❑ Discover ❑ American Express

Name _____

Organization _____

Address _____

City/State/Zip _____

Phone_____ Email _____

Card # _____

Exp. Date_____ Signature _____

Please make your check payable and return to:

BookMasters, Inc.
P.O. Box 388, Ashland, OH 44805

Call your credit card order to (800) 247-6553

Fax (419) 281-6883

order@bookmasters.com   www.atlasbooks.com